No Strings
Attached

No Strings Attached

THE SAVVY GUIDE TO SOLO TRAVEL

LESLIE ATKINS

Capital Travels Series

CAPITAL
BOOKS, INC.
Sterling, Virginia

All travel involves some risk. The author and publisher assume no liability for accidents, injuries, or other problems and difficulties, and caution travelers to become informed about safety and security.

Photography credits: Martina Bartel (p. 2), Lydia Goolia (p. 14), Justin Horrocks (p. 28 & p. 56), Valentin Casarsa (p. 44), Eliza Snow (p. 72), Shelly Perry (p. 86), fotoVoyager (p. 98), Christine Glade (p. 110), PeskyMonkey (p. 122), Tomas Bercic (p. 134), LongShot (p. 144), Aldo Murillo (p. 156), Vicki Reid (p. 168), Duncan Walker (p. 180).

Capital Books, Inc.
P.O. Box 605
Herndon, Virginia 20172-0605

ISBN 13: 978-1-933102-62-7

Library of Congress Cataloging-in-Publication Data

Atkins, Leslie.
   No strings attached : the savvy guide to solo travel / Leslie Atkins.
      p. cm. — (Capital travels series)
   ISBN 978-1-933102-62-7 (alk. paper)
   1. Travel. I. Title. II. Series.

G151.A85 2008
910.4—dc22

                                        2008013259

Printed in the United States of America on acid-free paper that meets the American National Standards Institute Z39-48 Standard.

First Edition

10 9 8 7 6 5 4 3 2 1

To my Dad,
for always telling me I could do anything I wanted.

To my Mom,
for her curiosity and interest in everything around her.

To my brother, Richard,
for the pursuit of creativity that we share.

To my niece, Rebecca,
for her love and affection.

To my friend, Payne,
for his enthusiasm.

To my friend, Hope,
for her encouragement.

To my friend, Gary,
for his support.

To my other friends,
for believing in me.

And for the many people I have met on my travels . . .

Thank you.

"The man who goes alone can start today; but he who travels with another must wait till that other is ready."
— *Henry David Thoreau*

CONTENTS

INTRODUCTION

Nothing compares to seeing it for yourself. Nothing matches the act of exploring a new place and meeting interesting and different people. In tasting the food, smelling the scents, and seeing the sites for yourself, you are able to filter and shape the experiences through your own personality and interests. As much as I travel, I also love reading or hearing about a place or an activity through the eyes and sensibilities of others—both those I know and those I don't.

I've come to accept that I can't go everywhere, be everywhere, see and experience everything. However, just as a good novel introduces us to characters we get to know through an author's viewpoint, so does a good travel story introduce us to a new part of the world and broaden our perspectives. Through sharing travel experiences, I believe we become better travelers who are more aware of the choices that are right for us individually.

I've traveled alone and with others—with friends, relatives, business associates, and boyfriends. I have enjoyed nearly all of my travels, even or perhaps especially, when things don't go as anticipated or planned. But I've become a savvy traveler mostly through individual exploration. For it is when you are dependent only on yourself, that you grow the most.

I've also become more informed and perhaps a more interesting traveler by listening and asking questions. As a journalist, some of this comes with the territory. I've learned to ask a question and then stay quiet, while the person I'm interviewing tells his or her story in his or her own way. It is in the details that someone chooses to share, in their turn of phrase or particular observation that a story comes to life. Prompting changes the story and thus is counterintuitive. This matters if you chat with someone at the next table in a bistro or across the aisle on a train.

I never realized I was skilled at this until I traveled with a friend who joined me while I interviewed a woman working for a well-known Parisian hotel. I would ask her a question, and my boyfriend felt compelled to answer the question. I've traveled with female friends who have done the same, who don't realize they need not interject themselves, who don't understand the interview process. So it is not a gender thing. However, it is important to know when to stay quiet—to allow the awkward silences to pass, to let the other person fill them or not, to choose their words and the direction of their thoughts.

In writing this book, I've spoken with a lot of people about their travels and noticed that many are apologetic. They haven't traveled as much as they'd like, they haven't left the United States, or they don't think their trips measure up to those of others. While there is always someone else who is thinner, richer, taller, or has visited more places for more days or spent more money or climbed a higher mountain, all of our travel experiences are unique and rewarding for different reasons.

If you get nothing else from this book, know that it is how your travel affects you that is most important. Whether you relaxed on a beach reading a junk novel, visited a local museum on your lunch hour while pretending— for just sixty minutes—that you were on vacation, climbed Mt. Everest, or trekked through the Sahara, the point is that you went, you saw, you conquered something for yourself.

That's why solo travel is an important component in everyone's life. It is not meant to replace travels with friends, families, and business associates. It is to complement those other travels so that in the process of getting to know our world just a little bit better, we get to know ourselves. Internal journey meets external stimuli. It is also ideal to go when your interests, free time, and business allow you a window of opportunity. I recommend that you open that window as widely as possible.

I've also realized that talking with someone about their travel interests and experiences sheds light on that individual's personality. When I teach writing workshops, I often recommend that in developing a character, my attendees get a fix on the character's bank account, make and year of the car that person drives, the section of the newspaper he or she reads first on Sunday morning, a favorite beverage, hometown, and more. Travel stories definitely bring to light important personality traits as well.

The first question someone asks a stranger is also telling. I've found this to be a geographic phenomenon. For those who live in Washington, DC, the first question is almost always about a person's profession. "What do you do for a living?" For those living in California, the first question is often about a person's hometown. "Where are you from?" All these factors define a character, and travel certainly belongs in the mix. I'm amazed how much I learn about people just by asking where they've been or where they want to go and why.

In the following pages, I'll share my ideas and experiences, as well as some I've borrowed from people I know or have met. Hopefully these stories will serve as a jumping off point for your own solo travels. Whether married or single, young or older, every one of us will at some time find ourselves somewhere unfamiliar by ourselves. It is to those moments that I say, bring them on!

—*Leslie Atkins*

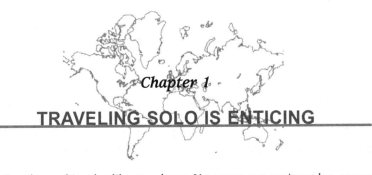

Chapter 1

TRAVELING SOLO IS ENTICING

Good travel is a lot like good sex. You start out on impulse, move with the mood, and hopefully find that the release is better than expected. As with a first-time lover who is as yet unexplored, you enter a journey as if it were an unfamiliar bedroom where you know your expectations will never match reality. If you're really lucky, both in the bedroom and on the journey, reality will surpass expectation. In any case, you learn things about the other person and at the same time learn things about yourself.

We are never exactly the same with two different lovers. Neither are we the same with two different journeys, even if the destination is the same. For the way in which we get there will be different, as time, experience, and particular situations color the experience a different shade.

With the freedom of letting go comes the risks and rewards that the routine back home will appear different through newly refreshed eyes. For those who needed glasses as a child, one never forgets that first moment when the prescription lenses are placed on one's face and the world looks clearer, as if having been through a giant carwash. Lines are more defined, colors crisper, smiles friendlier.

Travel similarly illuminates the world around us. We see clearer, for firsthand knowledge is not to be duplicated or replaced by however much reading or watching or listening we do. Twenty-four-hour cable news has brought the world into our living rooms and even into our bedrooms at night. Yet those are the details captured by someone else's cameras and reported through someone else's perspective. It is the details we glean from actually being there, from deciding for ourselves what to notice and what to ignore, that are unique to each of us.

Traveling solo is enticing and intriguing, like a new lover with the promise of thrills to come. One follows, perhaps a bit hesitantly, but so very entranced that any other path becomes hidden by the rush of emotions, the surge of adrenaline and hormones that say, "Come, come. You will be rewarded and ultimately satiated."

Of course, like the best sex, having a good travel experience just creates greater desire for "more, more." Perhaps not immediately, but soon, very soon.

What I am offering in this travel guide is the promise and conviction that the more travel you have and do, the more you'll want. Perhaps after a while, you'll be glad to go home—you'll miss the familiarity, the mundane, the people, even your job. But eventually, and it will not take long, you will look out over the horizon and wonder what's out there that you've yet to explore.

So proceed with caution, for travel, whether of the armchair or the wanderlust variety, is a lifelong preoccupation—a great one, to be sure, but not something to be easily left behind.

It is in the looking forward that we travelers thrive.

Having the Right Attitude at Any Altitude

Traveling companions, whether they are romantic significant others, best friends, or companionable co-workers, can be wonderful. With them, you share experiences, brave risks, and compare memories when the travel is over.

Yet there are times and instances when it is desirable or preferable to go it alone—to trust only yourself, to achieve something on your own, to recharge, to plot the next chapter of your life, or just to relax and unwind.

One of my friends does this with a rod and a reel on the shore of a river in a warm climate.

I've done it on the edge of a Maine cliff during a nor'easter. Although I was inside, the thunderous waves crashing against the rocks were still startling, still threatening, for my imagination led me to wonder if the walls of the hotel where I was staying would hold against nature's fury.

Sometimes circumstances cause us to go it alone—an intended fellow traveler has to work, we have a business trip, or there just isn't a friend available to accompany us where we want to go.

I've traveled with other people, often with great pleasure. It is a good way to get to know another person, even if you think you know him or her beforehand. Traveling in a new setting and different set of circumstances will change your perspective of that other person, even if it is someone you have known seemingly forever.

Yet I've grown more when I was on my own. I have been forced to talk to other people in my shaky command of French a nonexistent Italian. I've driven at night among moss-covered oaks on nearly deserted roads in South Carolina, my imagination running wild. I have listened to the endless waves lapping against the shore at the ocean, pondering important issues or nothing at all. On one memorable trip, I watched a fireworks display against the night sky from a ski resort in the Rockies, awed by the exquisitely clear air and the view of the lights dancing against the dark mountain.

At the end of a journey, one is never the same. You know more and feel more, having added memories to your collection—memories to be recalled later whether the experience was positive or negative. When you are "flying solo," this change seems to be greater. After all, you don't have the built-in comfort of an established relationship to protect you and keep you occupied. Since no one is there to hold you to your usual patterns, you can break those patterns. And because you can, you inevitably do.

> *There is a savvy way of going it alone, a way in which you will become your own favorite companion. In doing so, you will become a better companion to others too.*

Naturally, we want our travel experiences to be good ones. But sometimes the struggles, challenges, and mix-ups make the best stories—the ones we remember to tell our friends and children, the ones we think about in quiet moments that make us smile.

There is a savvy way of going it alone, a way in which you will become your own favorite companion. In doing so, you will become a better companion to others too.

Curiosity Leads to Good Interactions

When I visited Dublin, Ireland, I was surprised to find upscale shopping to rival what I'd seen previously in London and Paris. Ireland is enjoying great affluence, yet the sophisticated styles and high price tags still rather surprised me.

I had set a budget for my trip, and it quickly became apparent that buying the stylish clothes at an upscale department store in the shopping district would deplete my funds.

I decided to squander a precious hour of my trip to wander around the department store anyway, daydreaming of a time I might come back with more money. I'm one of those people who likes to look at merchandise I would buy if I ever won the lottery or inherited a fortune from an unknown relative.

I like playing this "what if" game in my mind. I enjoy living vicariously, imagining for a few minutes every once in a while where I would go and in what style I would travel if money were no object.

In reality, I am rather practical. Wandering around the Dublin department store, I found a beautiful but very expensive bed. I took a photo of the bed with my digital camera and decided to indulge myself with a pretty little soap dish—my nod to redecorating without a high price tag.

I've known people who are still paying for trips they took years ago. I never do this. I want my memories to be spurred by a thought, a photo, a souvenir, or a news item, and not by a recurring credit card bill that arrives month after month, or year after year.

I settled for the soap dish; the bed was just a fleeting thought. During the transaction, I chatted with the saleswoman who said she owned the bedding department as a franchise with her mother; they were renting space from the department store. She called her mother over, and we all had a long, very interesting chat.

I got to ask the mother about Ireland's role in World War II. Here, in the bedding department of a Dublin department store, I got to satisfy some of my historical curiosity. Why, for instance, hadn't Ireland joined the Allies in fighting Nazi Germany? Although pro-American, the Irish were so anti-British that they chose neutrality and maintained that stance throughout World War II.

Talking to the woman's mother, I got a glimpse into the intensity of emotion that went into her nation's decision. I have a bachelor's degree in European history, but I never experienced this kind of first-person account from my many college history classes.

The daughter invited me to join her and her friends later at a local pub. Unfortunately, I already had plans for that night, and I was scheduled to leave Ireland the next day. Had my evening been free, or my stay longer, I definitely would have taken her up on the offer.

Spending Only What You Can Afford

I try not to buy or spend money on anything I can't afford right away. This is particularly important when it comes to travel. After all, I've met people who took a trip to China, spent extravagantly, and then continued to pay for the trip years later on credit cards. That is not my idea of the appropriate memory trigger. Invariably, when you're traveling with someone else, money becomes an issue. I've learned to tip generously; I get real pleasure in the recipients' appreciation. Often when I'm with someone, I have to tip double because that person doesn't have cash or an inclination to reward service industry workers the way I do. When you travel alone, you set the budget and are not pressured to deviate by others.

Spending What You Need

On a trip to Mexico City, I was traveling with a friend who wanted to save money by taking the bus or subway instead of a taxi. I warned her that we needed to hold onto our possessions. As I sat a few rows behind her on a bus we took at her insistence, I watched a pickpocket finger my friend's American passport. I was able to thwart the theft by hollering at both of them.

Later, again at her insistence, we tried the subway during rush hour. It was unbelievably crowded in a way I have never seen elsewhere. Arms and legs seemed to be sticking out of the train's windows as it roared away without us, for I was backing out of the station through the crowd, pulling my friend with me.

Don't hesitate to pay for a taxi or even a car and driver while traveling. Perhaps this may seem extravagant. But I view it as a safety valve if I am unsure of where I'm going or how to get around. I view it as common "dollars and sense."

Having someone else drive is not foolproof, of course. Nothing ever is. In Paris on my own, I took an evening tour to the Moulin Rouge near Montmartre, figuring that would be a safe way of going out by myself for the evening. Instead of dropping me off at my hotel, as had been promised, the tour bus driver dropped me off somewhere else. I ended up wandering around a deserted part of a rather seedy *arrondissement*, or district, watching an unkempt man search through garbage cans.

Luckily, I was able to find a group of people having an after-hours party in a storefront. Although they didn't speak English and my French was iffy, one woman kindly volunteered a man she knew at the party to walk me the several dark blocks to my little hotel. I was truly grateful for this act of kindness, as I had been drinking champagne, I was wearing high heels, and it was really late. When the bus driver had complained about the narrow streets near my hotel and then told me we had arrived, I climbed off the bus without first looking around. The driver was derelict, or at least mistaken, but I was the one in potential trouble. I had a good plan for staying safe that night by taking a tour; it just went awry. By asking for help, I was able to remedy the problem. I don't know the man who saved me that night; I only hope my French was good enough to properly express my thanks.

Depending Upon Yourself

When you're on your own, you can make decisions about transportation and other measures. Safety in numbers is only true when your companions are at least equally savvy and risk averse as you.

As I did in Paris, ask strangers to keep you company for a few minutes if you fear that you are being followed. I am by no means paranoid. It's just that when you travel a lot, stuff happens.

A stranger can help even if he or she doesn't happen to play football or have a black belt in karate. The idea is that two people together are less likely to be a target. This is not to dissuade anyone from traveling alone, just to recognize that asking for help can make sense. I find people everywhere are anxious to help.

For some men who might hesitate to ask for assistance, remember that asking someone to help you, or to give directions, is tantamount to granting that person a gift. Most people, whatever their language, cultural background, or nationality, feel good about themselves when they can assist someone, especially a stranger who is sincerely interested in their culture and merely finds himself in unfamiliar territory. It is smart to admit what you don't know, but this requires tremendous self-confidence.

Learning the Hard Way

Being streetwise means doing whatever you have to do while traveling to thwart negative attention.

That first time I visited Paris, I was traveling alone. I knew I would be wandering around by myself and taking the Paris subway. So I dressed down, really down. I looked positively grungy, but no one bothered me—which was my desired result. I was determined to thwart negative attention.

While on the same visit to Paris, someone gave me a ticket to a fur fashion show at an elite design house. I wore the best clothes I had with me, which were not good. The most impeccably dressed and attractive people imaginable were in the audience. Now I make sure to travel with at least one nice outfit, even if my plans are just to "wander around" and go unnoticed. When traveling solo, you have the freedom, within reason and means, to change plans. You never know where you might decide to go or whom you might meet.

Whether you're a man or a woman, however, you should leave valuables, such as expensive jewelry, at home. You'll also want to safeguard your passport and money.

Thriving Outside Your Comfort Zone

I did some business by phone with a man in Dallas, Texas. Our conversation turned to the subject of travel, and he told me he marvels at solo travelers' abilities to go it alone.

He's been married a long time, he told me, and he's used to traveling with his wife. On a bicycle tour in France, he told me about a woman, an Australian, who was traveling by herself, and he wondered what allows people to do that.

He surmised that someday he might be without a spouse, and he sometimes ponders these things. Since I've never met him, I didn't pursue that part of the conversation.

"We all have a part of us that says we can be independent," he said. "What part, what exercise, is needed to say, 'I can strike out on my own'? How do you find that in yourself?"

We talked some more and agreed that one person's comfort is another's fear. I don't recommend taking on too much at one time if you're used to traveling with someone else. You might do better to try going solo for a day or overnight before you go off for a month on an extended African safari or to the Australian outback.

Part of doing something is sharing it with someone else. Another part is enjoying it for what it is.

Temptations

The man with whom I spoke in Dallas is obviously curious about solo travel. I could tell he finds it tempting on some level but intimidating too, probably because the unknown is always difficult even if it is also exhilarating.

The potential issues people mention when they're tempted to travel solo often fall into three categories:

1. *Loneliness.* You can also be lonely in a relationship or in a crowd. Or you can be fine by yourself. Circumstances constantly evolve. The only constant is change.
2. *Help making decisions.* This includes where to eat, where to stay, and what to do. It can be fun to determine what it is you really want to do without running it by someone else.
3. *Lack of feedback.* By traveling solo, you may be able to get in touch with your true feelings, find a new interest, gain understanding, maybe even discover extra spirituality, or just have fun. We're so used to being graded in school, evaluated at work, scored in sports, told we're winning or losing in the stock market. Why wouldn't we want our travels to be different?

If you must count, you can keep track of the number of states you've visited until you get to all fifty, or you can add up frequent flier miles amassed and amounts of money spent.

Alternately, you can live in the moment amongst people who might not speak your language, but probably have many of the same concerns as you—global warming, rising costs, a fight with their spouse, a new faucet for the kitchen sink, or a new winter coat.

You can sit at a bar, buy a cup of espresso, hike, bike, kayak, climb a mountain, lay on a beach reading a sexy novel, walk or drive across a bridge, or feed the pigeons in Venice's St. Marks Square. Even strike up conversations with strangers who become friends, albeit temporary ones.

What a Way to Go

Whether you are camping under the stars or beneath the roof of a five-star hotel, travel is a luxury.

It's an exciting way of being a student, too, whatever your age. After all, how better to learn than to go and conquer mountain climbing, snow shoeing, swimming with dolphins, or shopping where the salespeople all speak Russian and the prices are in rubles.

Education works both ways, so realize that you're an ambassador or teacher when you travel, even while you are studying everything new around you and trying to absorb as many details as possible.

Our culture and beliefs are part of us and are evident in such things as mannerisms and nonverbal cues, making travel a two-way street. The people we meet along the way are often enriched by our presence, even as they let us into their world to glimpse how they live. At the very least, those of us who are lucky enough to travel, must be humble and kind to the people we meet.

When you travel solo, you inherently talk to other people more than you would if you were part of a twosome or larger group. How you treat the people you meet, and what you choose to say, are that much more important.

Perhaps the village you visit is the only place the inhabitants there will ever know. Or maybe a ten-dollar bill given as a tip will feed their kids for a month. Maybe they have preconceived notions of an American from Texas or a Canadian from Quebec. Maybe you are the first traveler like you who they've met.

The allure of travel is built from the places we see and the encounters we have with strangers. There is value to conversation, even if we will never see or talk to the people again.

Tourism is big business in many places. But it is the chance encounters, the conversations, a smile, a door held open, directions given and received, language barriers overcome with hand signals and laughter, that weave a tapestry that becomes your personal travel experience.

On the island of Nassau, I took a short group tour in a van to give me a chance to look around. Due to a traffic jam, the driver turned down a poverty-stricken street. The tour guide grew agitated. Obviously, this glimpse of a poor residential neighborhood was not on the itinerary. But it is real exposure to the reality of such tourist destinations, and the ones I remember vividly, that provide balance. Perspective comes from real knowledge, not from selective sites chosen by a tour company. I was glad for the detour.

Be Careful What You Wish . . . You Might Get It
Many times that is a good thing.

Sometimes with travel though, it is an unanticipated conversation, a shop you happen to pass and decide to go in, a delightful meal in a cuisine you've never before tried, listening to television in another language, or getting to know a person you've just met—that may constitute the most precious elements of your travels.

Serendipity, karma, fate, happenstance—whatever you choose to call it—it is the unplanned that many times provides the magic. Plans are great, mainly because they lead to these unplanned moments.

If you knew exactly what would happen while you travel, you might go anyway. But it is the unknown that most challenges and satisfies our need for adventure.

We may choose to incorporate a certain amount of predictability in our travels. This may entail going to a place we've already visited, flying an airline on which we've previously flown, or doing an activity like golf for which we feel great passion and already know how to play.

But if you've never before played golf in Scotland, or flown into China and visited Beijing, or crossed a rope bridge in the jungle, there is one part familiarity and another part that constitutes the unknown.

We never know in advance all that solo travel will entail. Therein lies the thrill.

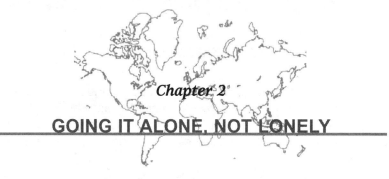

Chapter 2
GOING IT ALONE, NOT LONELY

There are people who go places. Actually, we all do, whether it is across town or across the continents. Then there are people who are travelers. As a travel writer, I get to go to a lot of places. Yet there are others I know who have traveled to many more places than I have, and some who have lived in other countries from several months to quite a few years—in places like France, China, Australia, Morocco, India, and Brazil.

There will always be someone who has been to more places or has been to those places longer, who spent more money or time, who took more photographs, or who talks louder or longer about their experiences.

I believe, truly, that it is the quality of your travels, not the quantity or distance that matters. Whether it's overnight in a motel or on a transatlantic cruise, on a day trip to Atlantic City or Las Vegas to play the slots or on a train trip through Siberia, a summer excursion to a nearby beach or on a safari in Kenya—it is your personal experience that matters. Naturally, the more you travel and the more exotic the trip, the more potentially interesting. But this is not necessarily the case.

Acting Like a Traveler
I've had epiphanies in mundane places. I've watched travelers try to top each other with where they've been and with whom they've talked. I've also been privy to a sharing of experiences among travelers with real love for adventure, with a genuine curiosity about the world and the people and places that inhabit it, and with those who have a desire to grow into the people they are meant to be. Travel fosters that, feeds it, transforms it, and, let's face it, makes the journey fun.

When I started writing this book, I spoke with people I met about their travels—much more than I had before. It's interesting, first of all, how everyone lights up when you ask where they've been or where they're going. Everyone has an experience, an opinion, a place they've been or somewhere they'd like to go. Their excitement is fascinating.

My mother grew up in New York City, so visiting Manhattan was a natural part of our lives. I recently met a man who grew up in Illinois and had just seen Central Park and Times Square for the first time; he was so excited by the experience that he couldn't stop talking about it. That same day, I met a woman who lived in Costa Rica for many years, yet she had only recently seen New York City for the first time, too. She was amazed at how easily she could get on a train or on the road and go to Vermont or Long Island. "I even thought of moving there," she told me, "but I'm not used to such a big city." She had lived in the jungles of Costa Rica, acquiring coping skills that would pose quite a challenge for many of us. Yet she found New York City, where I am always comfortable, to be a challenge. Talking to her was great, for it was such an interesting exchange—providing a way for me to peer inside her world and for her to glimpse mine. Where you've been and with what you're familiar certainly affects who you are and how well you adapt.

I am often surprised by the number of Americans I meet who have never been to another country. Apologetically, they admit this fact to me as if I am a priest, and they are at the confessional. At first I sought to reassure them. Then I switched to just listening to the reasons they've not been outside the U.S. and to their feelings about their lack of foreign travel.

Often they say it is because their spouse or significant other has less desire to visit another country than they do. Perhaps the person with whom I am speaking had grandparents who emigrated from their original homeland to the U.S., and they want to visit the place of their ancestors. Perhaps they are just curious about Africa or Rome or Rio. But they haven't gone, and their excuses are often shifted onto their spouse or partner.

Compatibility while traveling is an important facet of a relationship. Just as sex and money are issues, so too is where should we go and how should we squander our limited resources (whether those resources are of time or finances). Some people negotiate these issues better than others. Some couples take a break from one another—whether for a few hours or a few days—just so they can pursue separate interests on their travels and then meet back up again, all the more excited to see each other and talk about what each has done. There's no right or wrong approach.

After all, we don't stay glued to our roommates or spouses at home. We work, exercise, shop, go out with friends, watch TV, or play at the computer alone. So why, if we're away for two weeks, does anyone think that staying glued to one another's side twenty-four hours a day for fourteen days won't cause friction? Especially when we're used to a little alone time.

For those who would never dream of traveling solo, they might feel differently if they met the man with whom I recently spoke. He readily admitted that when traveling to Italy or elsewhere, he likes to sit in a restaurant and read the newspaper while his wife shops. He also likes to spend hours in a museum while his wife looks around for a few minutes and then wants to move on. They are visibly happy. They just spend a few hours apart each afternoon during their trips. At dinner, they catch back up. It makes sense to me, but of course, I like to travel alone . . . (though not always).

Then there was the woman I met during a group hike I took to see waterfalls on the north end of the big island of Hawaii. Her husband was off scuba diving while she pursued her love of hiking. She told me how her husband went off skiing in Colorado for a week by himself when none of his friends were able to make their annual ski trip with the "guys." For her part, she went without her husband on a road trip with friends; when no one in the group would go white-water rafting with her, she found a guide and went herself. "I was really hesitant," she told me. "But now that I've done it once, I would definitely do it again."

Footloose and Fancy-Free

Travel is far richer than merely getting from one point to another. As with much in life, the importance of a journey is often as important as the destination.

With this philosophy in mind, and since going somewhere always takes time, it makes sense to attempt to enjoy the road itself. This goes beyond the concept of traveling to see or do new things. How you get there, and your thoughts along the way, may be the most important parts.

According to one of my father's favorite authors, Louis L'Amour, in *Ride the Dark Trail*, "The trail is the thing, not the end of the trail. Travel too fast and you miss all you are traveling for."

There is great advantage to having goals and achieving them, knowing where you are going, and having a plan to get there. Often, however, the side excursions and unexpected detours can enrich the experience, and often provide a path that differs from your roadmap but may be more rewarding than the original plan.

Detours and side trips are easier to accomplish when you don't have to negotiate with anyone else. Stopping in a store, pulling over to the side of the road to take a photo or just enjoy the view, deciding to pair up with a stranger you just met, having a conversation with your neighbor on a train, or extending your trip to allow you to visit an extra city or country or just to stay put and soak up your current destination—those are the freedoms granted to us when we are exploring the world by ourselves.

> *Detours and side trips are easier to accomplish when you don't have to negotiate with anyone else.*

From minor details such as whether or not to sleep with the window open, or if you should turn the television on or off, to larger issues like the destination itself, the activities you pursue, the types of meals and entertainment you enjoy, or whether to run several miles or sit at a bar and drink a beer, doing whatever you want whenever you want is a great path to self-discovery.

Naturally, we all have responsibilities and commitments back home. But short of those, we have more control over our present circumstances when we're traveling alone. Ironically, it is this very control that inevitably allows us to let loose, relinquish or change some rules, and go with the flow.

I value traveling with others as well as going it alone. But it is important to approach each type of journey with a different mind-set, to maximize the experience, to see the world and meet the people in it through your own senses and perspective. To capture the thoughts and revelations and make them your own.

Fitting or Blending In

On my first trip to London, I met a man who invited me out to a dance club. In spite of the loud music, people kept coming over to ask me where I was from in the States. I was puzzled. After all, I wasn't talking, so they couldn't hear my accent or listen to my

American expressions and colloquialisms.

After this happened several times, I asked the next person how he knew I was from America.

"Your jeans," he answered. "They're American jeans."

Standing Out

"Have you been to the desert before?" I heard that question over and over. "Well, yes," was my initial response. "I've been to Las Vegas, Tucson, and White Sands, New Mexico." I was invariably greeted by vacant stares.

What they meant was, "Have you been to the desert here in Palm Springs before?" Or Desert Palms. Or one of the other towns in the Coachella Valley a few hours east of Los Angeles.

After a couple of days, I got it. To the people in this area and in L.A. and San Diego, the desert meant that valley. At least, it's likely to mean that.

As a tennis fan, I'm familiar with Indian Wells, where a large tennis tournament is held every March. As a movie fan, I'm aware of the Hollywood playground of Palm Springs and surrounding cities like Rancho Mirage and Palm Desert.

But being there is altogether different. A sort of unexpected culture shock.

I know that I am typically East Coast in many ways. But I was surprised at how obvious an outsider I was when I visited the California desert, even before I said a word. I was reminded of dancing in the London club when I had wondered if I dance like an American.

Here I was in the United States and still everyone seemed to know that I was from somewhere else. I finally asked someone how they knew and got an immediate answer. I was told it was my Nikes.

"My Nikes?"

It turns out that California girls wear only sandals or flip flops, especially in the summer.

So I switched to sandals and then everyone thought I was from L.A. I asked why and was told that my top was not as loose fitting as those worn by residents of the desert. They also said I was obviously sophisticated because I was wearing jewelry.

I wasn't wearing much jewelry, but apparently in the California desert they wear loose clothes and little else.

More on Clothes

At lunch with some Brits in London, they told me they can spot an American right away. I wanted to know how. It turns out that we wear our sweaters tied around our necks rather than around our waists to cover our "bums."

And we wear running shoes or "trainers" (at least if we're from the East Coast), and we wear black shoes (at least some of us) with blue jeans. They think that's pretty funny.

They also said Americans think they're inconspicuous by wearing a fanny pack or "bum bag." Actually, I learned this one a long time ago—that it's better when you're traveling to wear a vest with zippered pockets or a backpack. They're much less obvious than a fanny pack, and you won't stand out as a tourist. When you're hiking though, a fanny pack is still a useful accoutrement.

There's an entire art and science that makes up the fashion of travel, complete with its many implications.

In Hawaii, for example, if you are a woman and want to fit in, you must wear a bikini. For a man, board shorts are *de rigueur*. My friends in the Aloha State tell me that Hawaiian formal means that the woman is wearing a traditional flowing dress or mu'u mu'u, which does not have to look like a tent but can actually be form-fitting. Her husband wears a matching print shirt. In this way, it is obvious that they are together. One of my friends tells me that when she sees her husband, she thinks, "Oh, there he is—I must run the other way." It's a joke, but there may be some truth that the matching outfits serve as a warning to other people: "He's mine, or she's mine, so keep away."

As in California, sandals are ever-present in Hawaii, where going barefoot is perfectly acceptable too.

Avoiding Quirks

We all have them—those little idiosyncrasies that either endear us or cause others to have issues with us. Upon hearing I was writing this book, a married woman I know told me, "We all have quirks. When you're married to someone, you learn theirs. When you travel with someone else, you never know what you're in for." Then she told me the story of a recent trip she took with a former college roommate.

"When we got to the condo we were renting at the beach, my

former roommate ran inside and announced that since she had made the reservation, she would take the larger room with the ocean view. "Then when we went down to the beach, she brought along all her jewelry and other valuables and asked me to watch them. I refused, so she never went into the water the entire week because she stayed on the beach watching her things. I told her to lock the valuables in the car or in the room, but she wouldn't do that."

Towel, Please

I've personally traveled with a friend who uses every towel in our hotel room without leaving even one for me to use. On one trip together, I finally said something to her. After discussing it, we made a deal that she would leave one clean towel on the back of the door, just for me.

Luckily for our friendship, hers is an idiosyncrasy that doesn't bother me; I can always call the front desk to request more towels. I just find it intriguing that someone would actually use all the towels when they are rooming with someone else. But then, I'm sure I have some annoying characteristics too. I'm not aware of them, but I know they must exist.

There are no rules when you're by yourself.

Raising annoyances to a fellow traveler isn't always easy. In this case, we are good friends, so it is okay for me to joke about the towel thing. Humor is always a good diffuser.

Traveling solo, you can use every towel and washcloth and bar of soap. If there are two beds in the room, you can mess one up by taking a nap or eating in bed, and then sleep in the other one. There are no rules when you're by yourself. Just leave an extra tip for the housekeeping staff if, by indulging your fancies, you've made an added mess.

More on Quirks

What do you do when the quirk is your own? A New York City friend recently told me that he finds traveling alone attractive, and he has no issues with it. He does worry, however, that he is likely to waste time. "I'm less likely to put myself on a schedule when I travel solo," he told me, "which can lead to all kinds of mistakes." I would never characterize a person's travel style as "a mistake"—it's just their style.

Still, for my friend's benefit and for others like him, here is a plan for making sure you don't let all your days and nights go by without doing much of anything. I am one of those people who prefer it when no two days are exactly alike. I also firmly believe that a certain amount of do-nothing time is good for the spirit. But no one wants to miss everything.

If your style includes a rigid adherence to schedules, or if you are obsessively regimented, you don't need a plan to avoid wasting travel time. However, most people are attracted by opposites, so if this is not useful to you, you're bound to know someone for whom this will be vital information.

A Primer: So You Don't Waste All Your Time
Initiating Conversation
This is about interacting with people through conversation. The first step is to make a dinner reservation for a particular time. Your goal, if you choose to accept it, is to strike up three different conversations with three strangers and make them last at least fifteen minutes each. This can be done at a bar, on a beach, in a shop, or on the street. They can all occur in the same place or three different spots, but all three conversations must take place before you dress for dinner.

Conversations at dinner are optional, and they don't count toward the required three conversations. If you're somewhere that you don't speak the language, pointing to a phrase book and drawing diagrams or using hand signals will count, as long as the encounter is at least fifteen minutes in duration. For the rest of the day, you can do whatever you want—including doing nothing at all.

Keeping Track
Wear a pedometer all day and track your steps. You must take at least 5,000 steps daily; 10,000 are even better. You can do this by pacing up and down your hotel room if you want, but my guess is that your room or even a suite will get old quickly, and thus this preoccupation with taking many steps will force you to go out. Taking steps forward is also a metaphor for going places in your life.

In my personal pedometer frenzy, I've taken to wearing the little device at my waist at all times. I've even tried wearing a pedometer to bed. I figured that I might dream about climbing a mountain, and I wanted to capture every movement. Going to bed with it didn't work, of course. However, going to the door to let in room service might be worth a dozen or so steps, depending upon the size of your hotel digs.

An aside: With everyone constantly checking cell phones and BlackBerries for messages, a pedometer gives me an additional device I can check for those times when no one is calling, texting, or e-mailing me. It's called fitting in, not unlike when I jokingly told people I got a golden retriever so I could talk to myself and have other people think I was talking to my dog. (I really love dogs, especially goldens, so I was just kidding!)

The point is that humor is an inherently good approach for traveling alone. Whatever you do, don't take yourself too seriously.

Morning Room Service

I'm a night owl, so I'm much more likely to eat a late-night snack than a hearty breakfast. Left to my own devices and without someone along who likes mornings more than me, I love sleeping in. But who wants to waste precious time sleeping while you're on a beautiful island or in a fascinating city?

One of my favorite tricks is to order room service for early in the morning. Most hotels leave those long narrow door hangers on or near the bed during turndown service so you can order breakfast when you're too tired to think straight late at night. This can get expensive if you're on a budget, but at the very least, you might splurge by having coffee or tea and juice delivered to your room.

Sometimes the person delivering the food is cheerful that early in the morning, sometimes not. Usually the process of putting the food down involves my moving something else from off a table, and it certainly requires donning a robe and proffering a gratuity or signing the check. By the time all this takes place, even if it's just been a few minutes, I'm wide-awake. This technique works much better for me than wakeup calls and snooze alarms. As a tea drinker, I then have the hot brew handy with its requisite caffeine.

Afterward, I'm ready to hit the streets in search of something interesting to do. Or to find a proper breakfast if I'm so inclined.

Switching from Day to Night

If you're somewhere with an active nightlife, decide that for one day, you'll skip the sightseeing and museums and bungee jumping. Instead, get a massage or a haircut and go shopping for a new shirt or shoes to wear out that night. Take a siesta and then go out on the town in your new clothes, which will double as souvenirs when you get them back home.

If you've wasted part of the day in the process, so be it. You'll make up for it at night. You might try taking a ghost tour at dusk to jump-start your adrenaline. A concert or show is always good for nighttime entertainment too. If you're in Milan, try to catch an opera. If you're in Vegas, Cirque du Soleil performances can be found in several hotel showrooms. If you're in New York, you might see a show on Broadway, or in London try a theater in the trendy West End. You can always go dancing or bar hopping, or hang out at a café or in a bookstore. It doesn't matter what you choose to do as long as you're out and about after dark.

Planning a Nap

If you're somewhere warm with a beach nearby, get up early and plan to take a nap in the sun later. Just remember to wear plenty of sunscreen. You may not end up taking a nap, of course. But for those of us who like our sleep, knowing that you can catch more later is a great impetus for getting up early.

Taking a Short Tour

Taking a quick, two-hour guided tour by bus or in a private car with a hired driver does not impinge on your individuality or keep you from forging your own path. It does give you a great opportunity to see what's out there to be seen. You might decide to go back and explore inside the State Hermitage Museum while in St. Petersburg, or purchase a watch on the streets of Singapore. If nothing else, you will have seen Buckingham Palace from the outside, the obelisk in the *Place de la Concorde* and the Eiffel Tower, or Tiananmen Square.

If you're going someplace like St. Petersburg, you might want to schedule the tour in advance to make sure you can find an available one given in English at the time you want. If you're going someplace like Savannah, Georgia, there are so many tours each day, that you can make this a spur of the moment decision.

Taking a Lesson

Sign up to take a lesson. This can be in anything you want to try, or something you want to improve, such as body surfing, tennis, skiing, golf, windsurfing, bungee jumping, fly-fishing, or kayaking—you get the idea. While you might not spend the entire day doing the activity, at least for the hour or two of the lesson, you will have had the experience. This can turn into a great photo op, and it makes great copy for a postcard or an e-mail home.

After your lesson, try a new restaurant for lunch, and then treat yourself to a ten-minute shopping spree. You're allowed to buy anything you can find in ten minutes as long as it's under $100 or its equivalent in another currency. If you want to spend more, I want you to think about it for more than ten minutes. But for $100 or less, go for it.

TIP

Never (well, almost never) hesitate to hand your digital camera to someone nearby and ask him or her to take a photo so you get in some of the shots. Later, you'll be glad you overcame any reticence you might have to impose on a stranger. Keep in mind that most people love to be asked to take your photo—I don't know the reason, I just know that this request inevitably triggers smiles all around, and often, if you're approaching a group, there's a jockeying for who will be the designated photographer.

You'll be happy that you are there in the photos for posterity—not to mention, your own personal memories. On skis or with a tennis racquet in your hand, or perhaps crossing a river in the jungle by way of a rope bridge, trust me, you'll be glad that you're in the shot.

Do be careful NOT to hand over a camera to just anyone who approaches you and volunteers to take your photo. While you walk to an ideal spot in preparation for the photo op, the photographer might just start running away with your camera.

Been There, Seen It, Done That

I've been to the White House, Eiffel Tower, and the Statue of Liberty. I've seen the Mississippi River, the Las Vegas Strip, DisneyWorld, the battlefield at Gettysburg, and much more. Anytime I see a movie set in one of these or some of the other places I've visited, whether it's a drama or comedy doesn't matter—I have a visceral reaction to a location I recognize, in addition to being intrigued by the story. Since I've actually been to some of the places depicted, I can imagine the story in a way that enhances the movie experience.

There are many thrillers that incorporate the Pentagon building, for instance. One of my favorites is the old, *No Way Out*, in which Kevin Costner is trapped in a drama that unfolds at the Pentagon. Anytime I drive by the Pentagon building in Northern Virginia, I automatically think of the chase scenes from that movie. I've never been inside the military complex there, but I feel as if I have after seeing the movie many times over the years.

One of the reasons I'd like to go to South Dakota, perhaps the only reason, is that I'd like to see Mount Rushmore for myself, having seen Cary Grant and Eva Marie Saint crawling around on the face of a Hollywood replica of it many times while watching the classic Hitchcock spy thriller, *North by Northwest*, on TV.

Besides the film lore and movie memorabilia related to certain places, literary tours are also becoming more prevalent. In Europe, *The DaVinci Code* and *Angels & Demons* tours are popular. In Savannah, you can take *Midnight in the Garden of Good and Evil* tours.

A friend told me that when she arrived in London recently, she felt as though she were in one of the Harry Potter movies, having seen all of them with her kids. "Horns honking, cab drivers yelling— it was all charming, all kind of fun," she reminisced. "It was as if I were back one hundred years, as if I were sent back in time. I thought, 'my kids would love this.'"

Imagine if my friend took her kids to King's Cross Station, the London rail station where J.K. Rowling placed the magical "Platform 9 ¾" so that young wizards and witches could board the Hogwarts Express.

Specialty Tours

Whether it's a ghost tour in Charleston, South Carolina, an insomniacs' tour in Baltimore, Maryland, or a Jack the Ripper tour in

East London, you don't need company to enjoy specialty tours. There will be other people on the tours, too, so it's not just you and a guide; this cuts costs and allows you to enjoy the outing without being the center of attention. Thus you can enjoy being an observer. These excursions should be taken for a combination of entertainment and historical context, not for social interaction with others in the group, as that tends to be limited.

Although you may be walking about, the experience of such tours is relatively passive except for the charge of adrenaline you feel as you get scared or excited. If the tour guide is a good one, there will be drama.

Specialty tours are usually short—just a few hours or so, leaving you time to set your own pace again afterwards. Just having seen something of interest, with a particular premise, makes traveling a bit more appealing in an easy-to-achieve way.

Another recommended alternative is to take a one- or two-hour general tour of a city to get your bearings and see what there is to see, as suggested above in the "how not to waste time" primer.

Truth:
A path well chosen may be one that has been
traversed by others before you.

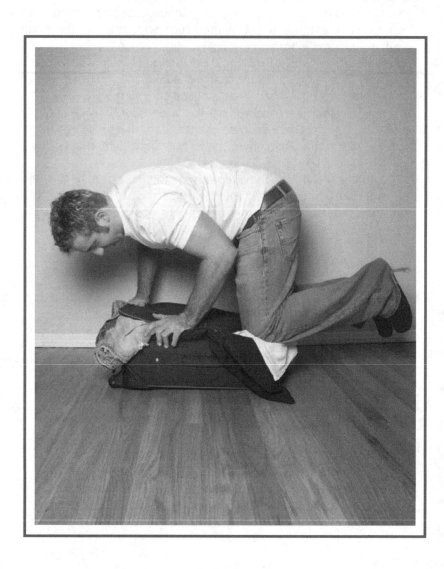

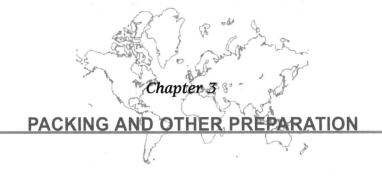

PACKING AND OTHER PREPARATION

Having the right mind-set is key. Traveling—seeing new things and meeting new people—is stimulating and exciting. If you want to stay home and hibernate, as you learn in the stock market, there is a time for bears. But if you want to be bullish and go out into the world, there's a time for that too.

Getting Ready Physically and Emotionally

Be honest with yourself. After all, the key to traveling solo the right way is in making your traveling companion happy. Since you're going to be traveling on your own, that means satisfying yourself.

Be honest with your family and friends too. Convince those who love you that you still care about them, that traveling on your own does not change that. You just want or need this time to explore by yourself. Or you're going on a business trip anyway, so you might as well visit a museum or catch the seventh game of the World Series while you're there.

If done right, you'll be a better traveling companion the next time you set out to travel with someone else. You'll also have a much better handle on what pleases you and what you can let go. Besides, it's bound to be fun or enlightening or both, and that's always a positive outcome.

Where you go is up to you, your budget, and time constraints. But comfortable shoes are vital for making sure you have a good time. You want to be as healthy as possible too, so get plenty of sleep for a week or so before the trip, eat well, and generally have your act together.

Many of us figure we can get rested or relaxed once we're away. However, it's better to start out calm and at your best, which means rested. It helps prevent the scenario, "I need a vacation from my vacation."

It's also a good idea to leave a day of relative ease for your first day back to unwind and unpack, as well as to reorient to your normal routine. This isn't always possible, of course. And, if your travels are satisfying, they may spark adrenaline rushes that leave you wound up rather than unwound.

Both ends of the spectrum are good—being excited and charged, or calm and relaxed—it just depends in what direction your search leads you. Travel is never exactly what you expect, so you can't always plan your probable reactions. Remember, it is the unknown aspect of taking a journey that is one of its best charms.

Know That You're Never Totally Prepared

You can never be totally prepared for what you'll experience while traveling.

However, if you like to travel, especially if you like to travel outside the country, rule number one is to keep your passport current so that you're prepared to go even if you're not prepared for what you'll find along the way.

U.S. passports are generally good for ten years, so keeping yours current is not something you need to do often. I noticed that mine was about to expire this year, and I put notes all over my calendar for several months in advance—"get passport photos taken," "renew passport," "passport expiring in two months."

After getting my hair cut and wearing my favorite color red, I had my passport photos taken. Then life intruded—my consulting business was busy, I had a trip planned to Palm Springs—there were lots of excuses for not proceeding with the process.

Since I'm a travel writer and often take trips on assignment at the last minute, I hesitated to mail in my renewal application. What if I needed to go somewhere while the passport was somewhere in process? I worried that I might not be able to track it down in time, or know how best to retrieve it. Bureaucracy loomed menacingly. So I procrastinated. I knew I couldn't get my passport renewed in person without an imminent trip at hand—the State Department's current rules won't allow it.

The unpredictable predictably happened, and I did have an imminent research trip to Stansted, England, outside London. My passport was due to expire a week before the trip was set to begin, so I needed to find a way to renew my passport quickly. (The State Department recommends that each citizen has at least six months left on his or her passport before leaving the U.S., since some countries require that much time upon entrance.)

After making an appointment by phone, I ended up spending an entire afternoon at one of the U.S. Passport Offices. My passport was in the last batch of passports processed that day. I managed to get mine renewed in person because I already had the photos, and my flight itinerary indicated that my trip was within the requisite fourteen days for anything other than renewal by mail.

I spent four hours waiting. I took an hour-long walk when they told me my passport would take a while. On my return, I managed to take a catnap sitting in a chair. The office had already closed to additional foot traffic, so I asked for, and got a pass so I could go out for a bowl of soup since I'd skipped lunch. Best of all, I spoke to interesting people who were also waiting for one-day turnaround.

One man was there with his father, who spoke little English. They were originally from Thailand, and his father was on his way back to attend his other son's wedding. When his father had gotten to the airport a few days earlier with other family members, he discovered that his passport had expired.

Oddly enough, in this day of terrorist threats, the man's son was worried because his father had packed a month's worth of his medications in checked baggage, which was already in Thailand, while his dad was still here. Yet security demands that bags only travel with their owners. Perhaps the bag was actually checked with his mother whose passport had not expired, and thus she went ahead; perhaps the medications were on the plane with her. Perhaps the story was not exactly right. Or perhaps security was not quite right. This is the stuff that makes up some travel stories—fact mixed with a bit of interpretation, or exaggeration, or confusion.

With a percentage of all checked luggage ending up lost, it is never a good idea to check needed medications or eyeglasses, night

---

TIP

Have all your travel documents in order. These include your passport, any needed visas, your tickets, hotel and rental car confirmation numbers, automobile insurance cards if you intend to drive your own car or a rental, traveler's checks, cash, and credit cards.

guards, shoe orthotics, or other similar necessary, expensive, and difficult-to-replace items.

A husband and wife, originally from Sudan, were also at the passport office. They were traveling to India but needed extra visa pages inserted into their passports. I didn't know that they stitch in the extra pages, so the woman showed me hers. They were still waiting for the husband's to be ready.

It seemed a veritable United Nations. There I was, getting my passport renewed, surrounded by people of many origins who are now U.S. citizens. I didn't have to leave the country to get exposed to some of the richness of travel. I just had to be in the right place at the right time.

Being Prepared

This is *very* important. Google.com, other search engines, and various travel sites are useful for obtaining information on just about anything relating to your travel. It does not replace, however, talking with people who have "been there and done that." You obtain different information when you talk to people you know and who know you.

The Internet is a major repository of information; but people can give you color, opinions, creativity. It's also a good idea to speak with people who are planning a trip but haven't yet taken it to see what ideas they might have to add to yours.

One friend told me I would love Ireland because of its citizens' propensity for telling stories. He knew that would appeal to me. You can't get that kind of personalized information online.

Aisle or Window

In addition to google.com, I recommend a website that is vital for air travel. There are lots of sites out there, and many of them are worthwhile. I can personally attest that this one is worth checking whenever you are booking a flight: seatguru.com.

SeatGuru is a fantastic website that allows you to input the name of the airline you intend to fly, add in the type of aircraft being used for a particular flight, and figure out which seats will be comfortable, recline, and have leg room; will not be too cold or noisy; will not be too close to the restroom or galley; and will have a window.

Whenever possible while I'm booking online, I check this out and then look to see the available seats on a particular flight before purchasing my ticket. I've changed flights and even airlines based on this information. When I've ignored SeatGuru's advice, figuring, "How bad can a bulkhead seat be?" I've been sorry. Now I listen to them.

Of course, an airline can switch aircraft at the last minute or change the configuration of the plane, or you may be electronically shut out of what appears to be an available seat. That happened to me recently—when what appeared to be a seat I would want eluded my efforts to choose it. I solved the problem by calling the airline after booking my flight online. The airline rep gave me an aisle seat up front, which is my favorite.

When traveling alone, you'll be sitting next to strangers, so seat preference becomes more important. I don't mind sitting by the window if a friend is sitting next to me and I can lean on his shoulder to fall asleep, or climb over him if I want to get out.

However, when I don't know the person, I like the freedom of the aisle, especially if there are three seats together. Being stuck in the middle between two strangers can be terribly frustrating, especially when the seats are small and the people next to you are either heavy or inconsiderate.

If you travel enough, you'll come across people with no airplane etiquette. I once sat next to a man who shaved in his seat, and others who encroached on my space. I've spoken with people who have been awakened on overnight flights when the people sitting behind them grabbed their hair or the backs of their seats while getting up to go to the restroom.

One woman told me how she negotiated with the woman in front of her when the woman's seat reclined into her lap. "I asked her to move her seat forward a little and she refused. Then I asked her to split the difference. She told me, 'I'll do it a little.' Do it a little and then do it a little more," she told her.

Luckily, people have different preferences. I like to sit towards the front because it allows me to watch what's going on and to disembark quickly upon landing. I know of someone else who likes to be in the last row because it is close to the restroom, he gets to board first, he can talk to the flight attendants, which he likes to do, and he can usually stretch out because nobody wants to be close to the restroom. He and I will never be caught vying for the same seat.

Climbing Kilimanjaro

Apparently this is not as daunting as it might seem on first blush. And you don't need to go mountain climbing to conquer a desire that seems intimidating but also appealing. We all have different, individualized versions of these challenging temptations.

Preparation is a large part of the process of "conquering the mountain," and this involves much more than just packing or looking for a deal.

A man I know proudly exhibits a photo of himself reaching the summit of Kilimanjaro on his office wall. We sat down one afternoon and he told me how I too could accomplish this same feat. Feat (and feet) are good descriptive words, for the process involves walking—self-propelled effort for several days up and a few back down. He trained for months in advance, preparing for the lack of sufficient oxygen and the physical effort of the hike up and back down the mountain. He was able to handle the climb up without assistance, but coming down was harder, and he needed help from one of the guides.

He told me how he met an older woman who was frail, but she had trained and made it to the top. "It depressed me," he said. "I was so proud of my accomplishment. Now I thought that perhaps it was not that difficult if this woman could manage it. The woman left her husband in Johannesburg after they took a safari, and she climbed Kilimanjaro in the care of hired guides."

The trick is to be well prepared. If climbing Kilimanjaro is your goal, it helps if you are in shape and have trained to become acclimated to higher elevations.

This man admits to being an "action junkie" who "needs things to keep me stimulated." He said he was getting older, and he "wanted to do something big, exotic, to combine physicality and travel.

"It never occurred to me to climb Kilimanjaro, but then an office mate suggested that I go. I was mildly skeptical, but my wife persuaded me. She has a taste for travel too. She pushed me up the mountain." He means this figuratively because she stayed at home with their children while her husband made the trip. Now it is one of his proudest accomplishments, so she knew the right thing was to encourage him.

Many great travel challenges require proper planning, but sometimes you can get by without planning. Like the time I was cold in Strasbourg, France, I was able to buy a wool scarf and gloves (which have since become great souvenirs). But no such shopping options exist on the way up Kilimanjaro. For that kind of journey, the proper outfit is important. "I made a crusade of it," said my friend. "Hudson Trail Outfitters knew me by my first name. I was either plying them with questions or returning things and trying new ones. It's important to dress in layers that keep you warm but do not cause too much friction when walking. I was told I would be climbing on wet, slippery snow at the top."

But he did not experience much snow at the top. "Perhaps because of global warming, it was not snowing when I was there. But there are glaciers at the top. And we experienced hard hail on the lower portions."

Other considerations include necessary shots and medications for altitude sickness, malaria, and a few other illnesses, with advance testing for adverse reactions.

The cost of such a trip need not be expensive, though there are varying levels of comfort. Add to the trek itself the expense of the airfare getting to Africa, a hotel at each end of the climb, and hiring the tour guides, as well as the cost of getting outfitted.

My friend wanted to extend his stay after the climb so he could take a safari at the nearby national park. "At the last minute, I couldn't arrange a later flight," he said, still disappointed a few years later. "I would have settled for anything—an extra day, an extra hour. I was on such an adrenaline high, I didn't want to leave."

On Packing . . . and Carrying Your Possessions

I've read all the articles and books and websites I can find on the subject of packing. I've also tried various suitcases, folding tricks, and list making.

I can synthesize it all down for you in a few handy tips:
- Take everything you absolutely need but nothing you can do without.
- Travel as lightly as possible. Even if a suitcase rolls, you may need to lift it into a car trunk, onto a train, into an overhead plane compartment, or onto a shuttle bus. Don't start out with a suitcase that's heavy when it's empty. Imagine what it will feel like full! This is especially important when you're

traveling alone. You need to be able to move quickly, and the fewer possessions you need to watch, the better. After all, there is no one to watch your stuff when you go to the loo (British for toilet), so you'll have to take everything in with you.

✔ Do not take expensive, irreplaceable items like jewelry and watches. Take a few inexpensive things that make you feel good, but only things that you can bear to lose or have stolen. Remove earrings and other items before falling asleep on a plane, otherwise they might fall into the seat mechanism, or fall off without you noticing.

✔ Leave sentimental items at home. Even if they are not monetarily valuable, they may be priceless to you.

✔ Be careful with laptops that have financial information that could help someone steal your identity. Be careful if you're traveling on business and carrying proprietary papers.

✔ Be careful with passports, cash, credit cards, and cell phones. Leave copies of your passport, driver's license, credit cards, and other information at home. If they are lost or stolen, you'll be glad to have the copies.

✔ Put your name and contact information on eyeglass cases, medicines, and other important valuables. This gives someone a chance to find you to return these items if the items are lost. Also, if you are robbed, these items will probably be discarded and someone who later finds them might want to return them. However, if your life is threatened, give these things up freely. Don't hesitate.

Just be prepared to beware. If you're not carrying anything that you can't bear to lose, then protecting those items will not be that stressful. Take some money with you and leave the rest of your valuables in a hotel safe. If there is no safe in your room, see if the hotel has a safe deposit box that you can rent during your stay. It may be worth the money and save you many hassles to have your valuables protected.

ALWAYS have zippered luggage, backpacks, and purses. A flap is not sufficient. If someone has to unzip or unsnap, they may go onto the next person who provides an easier target. Not that you want someone else to be a victim, but all you can do is stay alert and protect yourself.

Luggage

No luggage is perfect. That said, luggage gets lost, stolen, dirty, and broken. It's nice to have attractive luggage, but you must be realistic that having it is not a permanent arrangement. Consider that carefully before you spend a lot of money. You also don't want to appear too affluent, especially when you're traveling solo for it can invite the wrong kind of attention.

However, you will want to spend an adequate amount to buy decent luggage. Nothing is worse than a suitcase with wheels that don't work properly, making it hard to haul. If a wheel actually breaks, as happened to a doctor friend of mine, you will end up carrying the luggage the entire trip. I've had inexpensive wheeling bags with handles that ceased to retract, causing me problems on flights, as well as in the trunk of a cab. If a bag seems to be on its last leg, I retire it before it causes me any havoc. Of course, sometimes there's no warning.

Lost and Found

I recently found a black leather fanny pack on a hook in a ladies room stall at Stansted Airport outside London. Inside was an American passport, a London transport card, British pounds, American dollars, and some other items. I briefly glanced through the bag, took it out of the ladies room, and gave it to an official who promised to return it to its owner.

But I was nervous walking across the customs area with a lost pack, afraid that its owner might see me and accuse me of stealing it in a foreign country. I thought for a while before deciding to chance that by turning it in.

I've turned over lost wallets to the police in the States, always just a little worried that the wallets might have been stolen or lost during a crime. I turn them in anyway. But I know that in another country, you never know what might happen. Still, I felt good doing the right thing.

Had the owner of the fanny pack been more careful with her "stuff," she would have saved herself, and me, some trouble. I assume

> ### TIP
>
> *Besides paying attention to your possessions, attach a business card or other identifying information to your laptop, iPod, BlackBerry, chargers, and the inside of your luggage (in addition to the outer tags, which may break or become dislodged). By doing this, you make it possible that whoever finds the item or items has the ability to contact you so the items can be returned.*

the official returned the items to the owner, but I'll never know for sure. He said he'd make an announcement, and I waited around for a few minutes to hear it, but it didn't happen. Perhaps he checked and was able to learn that she had been through customs much earlier and was probably long gone. Perhaps he just didn't bother. No matter what happened, at least I did what I could short of trying to contact the person myself.

What to Take . . . or at Least Consider
A travel alarm. When I was in Palm Springs recently, I realized I had forgotten my travel alarm. I tried, as usual without success, to set the in-room alarm, but it sometimes seems like hotels buy clock radios in outer space to purposely confound guests.

I also asked for a wake-up call, but I was staying at a large resort, and my success at receiving these calls when requested is always variable. Besides, I need a snooze alarm and not all hotels are gracious in providing more than one wake-up call each morning. I can always count on the Four Seasons Chicago to call me two or three times, but their service is exceptional.

After two days of going without my travel alarm, I asked at the concierge desk for the best place to buy one, retrieved my rental car, and within fifteen minutes, I'd solved the problem at a nearby drugstore.

I recently struck up a marvelous conversation with a stranger on the train from New York City to Washington, DC. By the time I arrived in Union Station, DC, we had become fast friends, and she taught me to use the alarm on my cell phone. I had never before explored the "tools" button on the menu. As a backup to wake-up calls and my travel alarm, my cell phone is now a great new tool. The one I have allows for three different calls, in effect, a virtual snooze alarm. I've quickly learned that using a different ring tone from the one with which I get calls tends to break into my dreams more effectively than the tone I'm used to hearing when I get a call.

Flip-flops. The shoe kind, not of the political persuasion. Flip-flops can be worn as slippers in the hotel room, at a spa (even though they provide shoes, I like to bring my own just in case), while getting a pedicure, in a public restroom at the beach, on a hot or splintery boardwalk, in a fitness center shower (never, ever, go barefoot—fungus thrives there), at a pool, and these days in stores and at movie theaters.

They are waterproof, inexpensive, virtually indestructible, and highly versatile. An absolute must. Keep a pair in your suitcase and use another pair at home. That way you'll always have them with you.

Small bills. These should be in whatever currency is used at your destination. Keep in mind the currency exchange rate. In London, where a 10 percent tip is considered generous, I only had five- and ten-pound notes. When I had room service deliver tea to my room, I didn't want to give a tip that was equivalent to more than $12 U.S. So I gave the room service person a five-dollar bill and apologized for its being "American." I also made a mental note to get smaller denominations next time.

Going Light

A packing tip: if you can wash something, consider leaving any extras at home; this would include "extra" underwear, socks, and T-shirts. If you take a book along and you finish reading it, consider discarding it rather than carrying it home. If you buy something while you're away, consider shipping it home, but only if you won't be heartbroken if it doesn't turn up. (If it's a true find, you might be better off shipping your dirty clothes home instead and putting your newly acquired purchase in your luggage.)

Traveling with a little bit of extra space for the things you purchase is always a good idea. You might even consider bringing along an extra lightweight and foldable bag into which you can expand.

Layers. This is the answer to most situations. After all, it can be sweltering at 100 degrees Fahrenheit outside, but the air conditioning may be blasting on a train car or on a flight. If the heat doesn't work well in your hotel room and there's no robe provided by the management, you can always put a sweater on over sweats to stay warm.

Necessity Checklist

- ✔ *Passport.* Current with some blank pages.
- ✔ *Visa.* Not necessary everywhere, but it's best to check.
- ✔ *Medical provisions.* Includes eyeglasses, aspirin, and prescription medicines.
- ✔ *Immunizations and preventative medications.* Not necessary everywhere, but you may need protection from malaria or other diseases, depending where you'll be traveling.
- ✔ *Local currency.* Have enough for at least the first day; you don't want to have to change money immediately.
- ✔ *Travel documents.* This includes airline tickets, hotel confirmation numbers, and rental car or car service information.
- ✔ *Tech gadgets.* Cell phone, laptop, PDA, iPod, portable DVD, thumb (flash) drive, chargers, camera, extra batteries, and extra camera memory discs.
- ✔ *Credit cards.* It's a good idea to always have two cards with you in case you have a problem with one. This happened to me in Chicago. I used my American Express card in two hotels, one restaurant, and a department store. When I called home to check my voicemail, I learned that American Express had stopped the card because their fraud department determined that someone was using it besides me. I still had the card in my possession, but apparently someone had copied the number down and was using it to make charges online. I didn't receive a replacement card until I returned home a couple days later.

  While you don't want to carry a lot of credit cards, it's always good to have a backup. This is especially true when you're traveling on your own, as you can't depend on a traveling companion's card if something happens to yours. However, two cards should be plenty; if you have additional credit cards, leave

> **TIP**
>
> *Whatever you do, go light. When you're alone, you'll have to drag your possessions with you into the restroom, onto a train, into a taxi, or through the airport. You'll be the only one you can count on to watch everything and keep it safe, all while you're trying to see everything you can and absorb the atmosphere of this new, exciting place you're visiting. Even if it may be bleak countryside, it's bleak countryside you've never seen before so that makes it interesting.*

them at home. I like to carry my American Express card and either a VISA or MasterCard for backup.

✔ *Traveler's checks.* Cash is king, so these checks allow you to always have some on hand. Whenever you need more cash, you can refresh your supply by cashing these in.

✔ *Plastic zip-lock bags.* Indispensable for carrying liquids and gels onboard a flight. They also work well for a wet toothbrush, paper receipts, business cards, and a myriad of other items. I take extras because the zippers do break and I always find a new use or two on each trip.

✔ *Watch.* You've got to know the time.

✔ *Walking or running shoes.* Your feet need to be comfortable for you to be comfortable. You can also stay fit while on the road.

What to Keep Packed at All Times

✔ *Business cards.* These come in handy even if you're not on a business trip. Leave business cards inside your luggage, inside your eyeglass case, and in anything else you would want returned if it gets lost or stolen. Cards are also a good way of exchanging information with people you meet in your travels and with whom you want to keep in touch.

On a business trip to San Antonio, I accidentally left my business cards home. I had to call my boyfriend and ask him to ship my cards overnight via Federal Express. A day later and some forty or so dollars of shipping expense, I had my cards and a lesson learned. Now I leave a supply in my carry-on at all times; I've never forgotten them again.

✓ *T-shirt and a pair of jeans or sweats.* This is self-explanatory.
✓ *Underwear and socks.* If you'll be traveling extensively, plan to wash these out somewhere so you need not take too many pairs.
✓ *Pen and paper (or a journal).* We all have precious thoughts and ideas. You'll want to jot them down.

Change of Clothes

It's always a good idea to go light, but this is especially true when you're on your own. Without a friend or significant other along, you can sleep in a ratty T-shirt or wear the same jeans several days in a row, and who's to know.

Always bring along something to change into if you meet someone with whom you want to dine or travel around. One of the best things about being on your own is the freedom from having to impress or attract another person or persons, on whatever level you would have done that. Being a little grungy also serves to discourage being the victim of theft. Still, you want something decent to wear in case you run into someone you do want to impress, or if you want to go somewhere nice on your own.

Knowing you're going to be living in the same clothes for days or weeks at a time, bring clothes you either really like or ones you don't mind discarding along the way if you find others you want to purchase while you're in a new place.

I've made many mistakes packing and preparing for trips. These mistakes always teach me better ways of getting ready—the tips and tricks I've shared here. You can play it smart by learning from the mistakes I've already made. Each time I travel, I'm just a little bit better prepared because I keep learning something new.

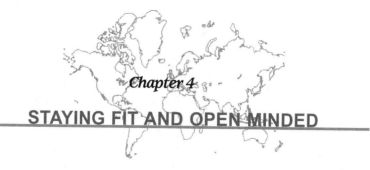

Chapter 4

STAYING FIT AND OPEN MINDED

The night before I take a trip, I invariably stay up late paying bills, doing laundry, and packing. As a result, I end up tired, with more weight in my luggage than I need or would have carried if I'd had extra time to pre-pack and then pare down.

The following list is a bit of "do as I say and not as I do." I'm working on developing new habits, so this is what I plan going forward.

For background, I've been lucky to land a few consulting jobs that lasted about six months each and entailed traveling out of town on a weekly basis in the company of experienced road warriors—those men and women who work on the road for months and years at a time, returning home on weekends.

Seasoned travelers invariably travel lightly, always keeping a bag half packed with necessary items like a razor for shaving and a pair of running shoes. They learn shortcuts to the airport and the best places for coffee. They know all the ground transportation options too and are experts at maximizing frequent travel points.

Road warriors are savvy, in their own way. But even they can use pointers for adding leisure to their trips, as they tend to be focused and—though flexible in the sense of changing schedules or flying off on the spur of the moment—set in their ways. As are all of us. To get the most out of any journey, whether for business or pleasure, it's best to be flexible—to travel light, to travel healthy, and to travel with an open mind. That open mind extends to being flexible and receptive to cultural differences, as well as to ways of thinking or speaking or behaving other than our own.

Getting or Staying Fit While on the Road

Picture a typical scenario: You were up late packing, and you've already spent several hours driving, parking, and waiting in an airport security line. There's a line for the restroom and another at the food counter. All you are thinking is that you need caffeine and chocolate, so you head for the snacks at the newsstand. As tempting as that might seem, it's really not a good idea.

How should you stay relaxed and calm while also maximizing your fitness when flying? It's never completely easy, but it will be more so if you follow, or adapt, these ten tips:

1. *Drink lots of water.* Staying hydrated is key to reducing headaches and jetlag. It's advisable to drink water when flying—much better than alcohol while in the air. It also keeps you from eating so much junk food, which is usually just a result of boredom or nerves.

With airport restrictions on liquids, you'll have to ditch the bottle of water you brought from home and buy a more expensive one at the airport. It's worthwhile though—consider it a necessary travel expense. If your flight is delayed on the runway, you'll have something to drink, especially if you're flying coach. (In business and first class, they will give you something to drink before you hit the runway.)

Some people try to limit fluids to avoid trips to the teeny-tiny restrooms onboard. Within reason, it's healthier to stay hydrated. It's also good for you to get up and go to the restroom. Moving around helps prevent neck and leg cramps and helps avoid potentially dangerous leg embolisms, or blood clots.

2. *Move around.* Don't you just hate sitting next to someone on a flight who squirms around and keeps you from sleeping or reading in peace? That someone is actually smart, for moving around, stretching, even doing in-seat exercises is good for preventing a sore back and blood clots, as mentioned above. Just be as considerate of your neighbors as possible while you do your seated stretches and mild exercises.

Before you board the plane, don't just sit around the airport terminal. Stand, stretch, and move around. Look around the bookstore or the newsstand. You'll be sitting long enough on the flight itself. But don't wander too far. You don't want to miss your flight!

This happened to one of my friends. The airline announced that her flight would be delayed an hour. My friend went to get something to eat and returned about twenty minutes later. The waiting area was pretty empty when she got back, which was her first clue that something was terribly wrong. She went to the counter and asked about her flight. "Oh, that flight left already," she was told. Although they thought there would be a delay, the airline's plans changed rather quickly.

This almost happened to me once too, but some sixth sense told me to stay put; luckily, I didn't miss my flight when it boarded and took off as scheduled. My friend was not so lucky, and it took her fifteen hours to get from her home in Phoenix to her hotel room in San Antonio. She spent most of the day waiting for another flight at Phoenix's Sky Harbor International Airport.

3. *Give yourself a present.* Make it a steamy novel or crossword puzzle book, an iPod or portable DVD player. These items are better than a bag of Hershey bars or gummy bears. Many of us are budget conscious. But if an enticing read or favorite music will make us happier, we'll eat less, drink less alcohol, smile more, and have a better time. Endorphins, our "feel good" chemicals that release from smiling and laughing, will charge into our minds, making travel that much better.

4. *Do less before you leave.* I tend to act as if I'm not coming back, thus I try to get my entire life in order. Perhaps that stems from a slight fear of flying, although I don't let fear hold me back. Perhaps my trying to do so much before a trip also stems from a subconscious desire to be more organized, a secret longing to have everything in place when I get back.

Packing a day or two or even a week in advance makes traveling much less demanding.

Whatever the cause, I need to remember that a six-day trip is less than a week, a weekend is just a few days. The work, the bills, the laundry, and the gardening will all be there when I return.

Packing a day or two or even a week in advance makes traveling much less demanding. I like to keep my carry-on pre-packed with all my must-haves. I can then select my clothes at leisure, and double-check to see that I've brought everything I need but not too much. Over-packing is often the result of grabbing last minute items in a panic.

Years ago, on a trip to the French and Italian Rivieras with a friend, I packed at the last minute. When I got to Nice, I discovered three full-sized bottles of shampoo in the huge suitcase I had packed. Today I would discard all of them, but at the time I lugged them from town to town and then back again to the United States! My friend and I laughed about it for years afterward. While it is funny in retrospect, it was not so much fun lugging the heavy suitcase around.

✗ 5. *Pack snacks in your carry-on.* Do this on the way home, too. If it's a panino sandwich before you board the plane in Florence, so much the better. Boxes of raisins, peanut butter crackers, not-too-juicy fruit (so you don't make a mess), and your favorite kind of sandwich—are all possibilities, to give you some ideas. Don't forget to throw in a few napkins or paper towels.

On domestic flights, the airlines may prefer that you purchase their onboard snacks, but I've noticed that they tend to run out, and it's never what I want to eat either calorie-wise or energy-wise. I get a little nervous waiting for take-off too, so I like to have a healthy snack that I can access immediately. Often just knowing it's there is enough to satisfy my emotional need without my even eating it. On the theory that keeping a well-stocked refrigerator deters overeating, when you start running out of food, there's a tendency to eat more. If I'm stuck on a plane with no access to food, I don't like it.

Bringing along snacks will also keep you from the temptation of buying excessive junk food at the airport. Or drooling while the folks across the aisle devour the pizza they bought in the terminal. I once bought spareribs at an airport and ate them onboard a plane. I thought a couple of the passengers were going to mug me to get to my food. If I ever to do that again, I plan to buy extra so I can share.

6. *Pack lightly but bring a mini-pillow.* There's no need to buy an expensive mini-pillow; you can pick up an inexpensive one at Target or Wal-Mart. I first bought one to comfortably support my back while driving. I soon realized it was the same size as the pillows the airlines sometimes have available. By bringing along your own, it is always there, as the airlines are discontinuing pillows in many cases, and there are never enough for everyone.

Bringing your own pillow also ensures that it is clean. After all, why would you want to rest your face or hair against a pillow already used by travel-stressed and potentially germ-ridden strangers? Your own pillow is probably more comfortable and if you're inspired by appearances, you can choose one that comes in a pretty color. You can also use the same pillow on a train, in a taxi, even in a hotel room. I use my mini-pillow behind my back when I drive a rental car.

The trick is to remember to take the pillow along with you—after the plane lands, when you check out of the hotel, or when you return the rental car. There are distractions at all these junctures, so make a conscious effort to collect all your belongings. Worse case—you leave it somewhere and have to buy a new one; that's even more reason to make it an inexpensive one.

As a woman, I find it helpful to bring along a small, foldable fleece shawl that can double as a blanket. It is easier to wrap around yourself than a jacket while on a plane, train, bus, or car. Sometimes I just bring the shawl and bunch it up to put under my head for a pillow. A rolled up sweatshirt makes a good pillow too, especially for men. The trick to packing lightly is to learn to double-up on uses for everything you bring along. (When I'm by myself, I sleep in just a camisole or T-shirt, or if it's cold, I sleep in sweats that I can also use when working out.)

If you're flying internationally in either business or first class, it isn't necessary to bring along a blanket or pillow, as they will provide what you need to be comfortable. However, if cleanliness is a concern, bring your own. If you're attempting to upgrade but not sure if it will come through, you need to be prepared to fly economy. Snacks aren't necessary in first or business class either, as you'll be kept well fed. But for those who usually go by coach, especially flying coach on longer flights, these ideas are good ones.

7. *Bring workout shoes.* To exercise, you can always make do with clothes like sweats or a T-shirt and shorts that can double for sleeping. This is especially true when traveling alone because you don't have to worry about looking special for someone with whom you're romantically involved, or covering up for someone with whom you're not. But shoes are irreplaceable if you plan a workout, or even if you'll be doing a lot of walking.

On a trip to London, I wore a new pair of workout shoes to the airport. I hadn't broken them in and as a result, they hurt my feet. Taking my shoes off at security felt good, but then I had to squeeze back into them. I took them off again in the air, but each time I went to the restroom, I had to put them back on. Luckily, I had packed an old pair of sneakers in my suitcase; once I got to London, I was able to switch to the old pair.

Note to self: Next time, either break the shoes in ahead of time or leave them home. While I had the old pair with me, carrying both made for extra weight and space in my luggage, which really wasn't necessary if only I had planned more carefully.

8. *Walk, run, or jog.* Don't stop working out just because you're away from your exercise bike. Most resorts and hotels have fitness rooms, so there's no excuse for skipping a workout. Maybe the equipment isn't as good as what you have at home, but maybe it's better. Besides, sweat is sweat whether you're in Buffalo or Bangalore. You'll feel pride, get an ego-boost, and it's good for your heart, lungs, and legs. Even better is getting out of the hotel for a walk or run around the Eiffel Tower, down Copacabana Beach, or around Hyde Park. It's a great way to get to know a new city, and you might "run into" another energetic traveler with whom you can share some time.

9. *Two tiny additions to what you pack.* Take a stretch band. It weighs practically nothing and folds up into a tiny space. Before I go to bed or when I wake up, I like to use it to stretch my legs. My other recommendation is to take along a pedometer that hooks onto your waistband. I hardly ever go anywhere without mine anymore—it's become a must-have. If I walk close to the recommended 10,000 steps every day, I either lose weight or give myself the ability to eat anything I want without gaining weight.

If you wear a pedometer, you'll be surprised to learn how much you move about in an airport, shopping mall, or casino.

If you wear a pedometer, you'll be surprised to learn how much you move about in an airport, shopping mall, or casino. That may just prove to be enough exercise to have that extra scoop of gelato in Venice. But you won't know for sure unless you keep track of your steps.

A pedometer is tiny and lightweight. Between a pair of exercise shoes, a stretch band, and a pedometer—you'll be all set. If you prefer another form of exercise, by all means, bring what you need. But if you're traveling to a business conference and plan to sneak out one morning for a round of golf, renting clubs might be a better idea than lugging yours along. It will be much less obvious, and for just one morning out of an entire trip, it makes more sense than bringing your own clubs. Unless you're Tiger Woods.

10. *Private moments.* Take a breather—from work or even from interaction with a traveling companion. One married woman I met on a visit to Lake Austin Spa Resort in the Texas Hill Country told me that she was having a much better time at the destination spa without

her husband. "When we travel together, we're nitro and glycerin." Not all spouses are happier apart while traveling, but even a short breather will make you more relaxed and ready to conquer sightseeing or meetings. You'll sleep better too.

On the subject of sleep . . . take along a good book, something comfortable to sleep in, and climb into bed earlier than usual. Limit caffeine and alcohol, keep bottled water by the bed, and try doing mild stretches while counting your blessings. After all, you are lucky enough to be traveling . . . challenge yourself and enjoy the stimulation.

Integrating Cultures and Ideas

Cultures differ across the United States, not just across the pond (the Atlantic Ocean). I was totally convinced of this the first time I visited several pueblos in New Mexico. Here was a different climate, a different culture, and a different U.S. from that to which I had previously been exposed.

I grew fascinated with the Native Americans I met. They, like some of the people I met while traveling in Mexico, generally prefer not to have their photos taken. In some cultures, capturing a person's photo is equated with capturing their soul. I learned to be respectful and to ask if it is okay before I use my camera.

At the Taos Pueblo, I was told a photo was okay, but only if I paid $5. I assume it is just a financial issue there and not one of spirit; for although $5 is a lot for a snapshot, it is not nearly enough for the pricelessness of a soul.

New Yorkers reference "north of the city" as if there's only one city in the world. This is their shorthand for their hometown. Actually, people in other urban areas tend to do the same thing, but not quite to the same extent.

Then there are the expressions that are local. When New Yorkers talk of B & T, for example, they are referring to those commuters who must take bridges and tunnels to get into "the city" from New Jersey and Long Island. Even if you're traveling in the U.S., there will be regional and local expressions that differ from your own.

In New York, the candy on top of ice cream is referred to as "sprinkles." In Baltimore, where I grew up, they are "jimmies."

In Ohio, I once asked for a soda. The waitress asked me what flavor, when all I wanted was a Coke. It turned out that in Ohio, I needed to ask for "pop." When I asked for a bag for my Coke, the woman thought I was from outer space when all I wanted was a "sack" so I could carry my Coke out to the car. And on and on . . . In London, they call cola drinks "fizzies" or "fizzy drinks." I think I like that best.

Seduction on the South Carolina Coast

I've been to South Carolina a few times. The first time was with my parents and brother on a road trip to Miami when I was young. My main memory of the state was a boring ride on Interstate 95 peppered with billboards every few minutes hawking a place called South of the Border. It was a brilliant advertising ploy leading us to a place that served food and junkie souvenirs.

Later I went to Charleston for a lovely long weekend. My boyfriend and I stayed at a bed and breakfast, ate fabulous meals at various French restaurants of which there seemed to be many, and took a ghost tour at twilight. It was romantic and changed my impression of the state. Still, it remained one of those places that I'd visited, but not which I felt I knew.

Then I met a man from Beaufort (pronounced Bwew-fert). Beaufort is a small, affluent town situated on the South Carolina coastal marshlands and the shore of the Beaufort River. Its antebellum (before the Civil War) mansions were spared during the Northern War of Aggression, as the Civil War is called in some southern states. General Sherman reportedly had friends who lived in the town, and he made a deal to spare the place on his march of destruction.

My friend from Beaufort entranced me with tales of the beauty of the place, of its idyllic nature, of its very small "townishness." In going through my dad's old issues of *Southern Living* magazine, I invariably find mention of the town or a short article about some aspect of life there.

I pictured this tiny little place, and I couldn't imagine it would live up to my friend's romantic description—after all, what could? I grew up in a suburban neighborhood and have lived most of my adult life in an urban one. A small town was unfamiliar to me.

Beaufort is situated about halfway between Savannah and Charleston. On a trip to Savannah, I rented a car and set aside one full day to drive to Beaufort, just to see for myself. After all, my friend's stories were seductive, but I wasn't sure his descriptions were at all accurate. My curiosity got the better of me.

It turned out, that as I drove over a large bridge into Beaufort, I saw the marshes just as they are depicted in the film version of *The Prince of Tides*. The beauty of the area is legendary through film lore, for Hollywood producers and directors long ago discovered the picturesque town. *The Big Chill*, *The Great Santini*, and *The Prince of Tides* were all filmed, at least in part, here.

It's a literary town too, with bookstores featuring local authors like Pat Conroy, a branch of the University of South Carolina, and many history buffs. Great homemade ice cream is available near Waterfront Park. Double curved stairways on many of the historic houses in the part of town called "The Point" attest to an architectural history that provided separate access, even to residences, for men and women.

Beaufort is also a place to contemplate the seagulls that alight on the river, fish for spottail bass or seatrout in the marshes and from small boats, sit in Waterfront Park and eat a sandwich, or take a walking tour of the local mansions. There are bed and breakfasts too, if you want to stay.

I would never have known about Beaufort if I hadn't listened to my friend, would never have noticed the articles in those back issues of *Southern Living*, would never have spared a day of my short trip to Savannah to visit this town—the drive to which is filled with roads covered by drooping, moss-covered oak trees that add drama and melancholy to the drive. That melancholy is immediately dispelled the moment you set sight on Beaufort.

Theirs is a way of life different from mine. That is what travel is all about. That is the value of having diverse friendships, for in talking to others we learn about places and points of view divergent from our own. For just a day or two or a week, we can absorb unfamiliar places and points of view and change who we are just a little, letting in some things that are new—altering and expanding our point of reference.

Truth:

How far we go is not as important as how much it affects us.
The great gift of travel is qualitative rather than quantitative.
This is not a numbers game—it is transformational.

On Walking

When I was a little girl of about ten, I hated summer camp. I was homesick, and I didn't think much of the activities or the accommodations at the sleep-away camp I attended for a few weeks. However, there was one morning when we woke up before dawn and took a sunrise hike over the mountain in Western Maryland where the camp was located. The weather was great, branches breaking beneath our feet as we trudged several miles to look out over a valley as the sun began peeking through the sky. On a fire he built, the guide cooked the most delicious eggs in an iron skillet. That was it for me—a morning I will always remember.

I am a city girl now, living in a totally urban environment. Last year, when I visited a castle in the Irish countryside—Ashford Castle which was previously owned by the Guinness family—other guests made good-natured fun of me for being unfamiliar with the falconry and horses on the rural grounds.

Still, I happily walked around the property and appreciated the silence and grandeur of Lough Corrib, where I went out on the lake with a ghillie to learn to fly-fish. I learned only a little about how to cast, but I did come to understand the appeal of the sport, especially in such an awe-inspiring setting.

However, on that sunrise hike of my childhood, it was the moving through nature that so touched my sensibilities and charged my energies. Despite the fact that I now live in a city, or perhaps because of it, I walk outside every day, usually several times a day. It is how I keep fit, it is a means to gather endorphins, and it is my way of working out overwhelming emotions—whether they are positive or negative.

When I add the stimulus of an unknown or foreign place to my penchant for walking—then I am elated. I love to wander streets looking at florist stands and cafés, hike trails in the mountains, and create footprints in the sand by the surf. I love to wander around art museums too, and casinos where I enjoy watching people more than I like to gamble.

Whatever I am doing, wherever my travels take me, my preferred method of seeing places is by walking around. According to Henry David Thoreau, *"An early-morning walk is a blessing for the whole day."* That works, because I try to stay safe and thus there are places I don't choose to wander around at night. But after dark, in places where other people are around and my instincts say it is okay, I will walk at night too. J.K. Rowling notes, *"Nothing like a nighttime stroll to give you ideas."* So I mix it up and do both when I can. Why not?

On Personal Space

During a summer job while I was in college, I was teamed up with a man from the Netherlands. I found myself constantly backing away from him, because he liked to stand too close to me when we talked. This was the first time I realized how utterly American I am in expecting lots of space everywhere, including around me.

It is worth noting that there is a spatial impasse that often causes trouble across cultures. As Americans, we are from this big, beautiful country with lots of space. In urban centers, we might be more crowded. But we have vast uninhabited lands and semi-deserted rural areas. So we afford each other more space around ourselves than others do in smaller, more crowded countries. Perhaps that's why we're so uncomfortable on many elevators and planes—where we are forced into small spaces with our fellow travelers.

A few years ago, I had plans to meet a friend of mine at a bar in Detroit. When I got there, another man moved over to let me sit with my friend. I turned to the stranger and thanked him. It turned out that the stranger was drunk, and he kept moving closer and closer to me, getting in my space. So I boldly said to him, "You're in my space."

"What are you going to do about it?" he asked belligerently.

"I've got a great left hook," I responded, and then I started giggling. I didn't even know at that time what a left hook meant. Had I been alone, I would probably have moved. But since my friend was tall and strong, I figured he would defend me if I came to blows with the drunken stranger. In that situation, I had a lot of nerve.

If someone seems to be crowding you and they are not American, you might keep the cultural differences in mind. Understanding is better than throwing a left hook or a right jab.

If you happen to be sitting at a bar next to a belligerent drinker who is crowding your space, wherever the bar is located, it's probably smart to get up and move to another seat. Or put up with a bit of crowding.

Chapter 5

SURVIVAL, SECURITY, AND COMFORT

"*Men must know their limitations,*" said Clint Eastwood. Dirty Harry with limitations? Of course. We're human. We're tough and adventurous, excited and exciting, but none of us is good at everything. It is important to recognize that travel makes us vulnerable. We can get good at it, but we're still in unfamiliar places with people who don't necessarily speak English and who have different cultures, practices, politics, religions, food, and clothes. We need to adapt, but not so much so that we lose ourselves. Tricky, isn't it?

Nightlife and Laughing by Yourself

I called a hotel rewards program to book a stay at a New York City hotel using some of the frequent traveler points I had amassed. I began talking with the woman who worked there about travel in general and her experiences in traveling herself and in assisting the many callers she helps each day.

She told me that she remembers the first movie she ever saw by herself, including the actors who appeared in it.

That got me to thinking. I've gone to lots of cultural events—Broadway and off-Broadway theater, as well as theater in London's West End, opera in New York, the Cincinnati symphony, various ballets, Cirque du Soleil performances in Las Vegas, and much more. Usually I'm with friends or family.

But there was one time when I was in New York City by myself, and I bought a ticket to see a musical comedy. I remember thinking how funny it was to laugh out loud in the theater without anyone there with me. The theater was crowded, of course, but with strangers. It was then that I realized that we laugh and cry at these events, in part, as a way of communicating with the person or persons with whom we're attending a show. Laughing just for the sheer humor is a different experience. You soon learn that it is okay to be alone and laugh or cry at a play, to enjoy a ball game by yourself, and to see things through your own eyes without another person against whom to measure your reactions.

Having Fun . . . but Being Wary

A similar thing happened to me when I went to Bermuda for a five-day holiday. I was hesitant to go there alone since I thought of the island as a honeymoon haven. What would I do by myself in the middle of cuddly couples? A man for whom I did some writing loved going to Bermuda as he enjoyed playing tennis there. He encouraged me to go, even recommending a guesthouse rather than one of the large hotels.

What a great little sojourn those five days turned out to be. First of all, Bermuda is a really manageable island. I rented a moped, even though I am afraid of motorcycles. I just did it without thinking since it was the most feasible way of getting around.

I met and went out with three men while I was there (on different nights). The men were on business and were glad to meet a woman traveling solo. One thing I wouldn't do was to get into a car with any of them, so we went out in Hamilton, one of two major towns on the island (along with the quieter St. George), where we could walk from my guesthouse. My instincts told me not to trust getting into a car with a stranger, even if it was a taxi. I've learned to trust my instincts, even if I err on the side of caution.

I've learned to trust my instincts, even if I err on the side of caution.

The other thing that happened in Bermuda was my epiphany about dining out. The guesthouse where I was staying had its own restaurant. Breakfast, afternoon tea, and dinner were included in the cost of my stay.

The first night at dinner, seated in the charming restaurant with a view of the inland waterway, I looked over the menu and was stumped. There was no one with me to say, "What looks good?" or "What are you going to have?" or "I think I'll have the . . . whatever."

As a result, I sat and studied the menu as if I had a final exam on it the next day. Finally, the waitress came over. Potato leek soup was a special. I had never had it before, and I didn't know anything about leeks—me, a gardener's daughter. But my dad had never grown leeks.

He had grown spring onions and zucchini, all sorts of tomatoes, strawberries, and pumpkins, but no leeks. The waitress explained them to me, and I decided to try the soup. It was delicious. I have since tried grilled leeks and all sorts of other dishes made with leeks. Sometimes I'll order an entrée just because it is accompanied by a side order of leeks or prepared with leeks. I love the taste. And I never fail to picture myself at that guesthouse restaurant in Bermuda. It is such a pleasant memory, and it has enhanced my culinary taste while enriching my life. I eat out a lot and seeing leeks on a menu is just one of those threads in life that is woven into the fabric of who we are; it's a little thing but the little things add up.

Staying Safe . . . Street Fights and More
The first time I went to Paris, France, I went alone. A travel agent booked me into an inexpensive hotel in a rough *arrondissement* (an administrative district) populated by mostly immigrants. It was not a good section of the city, and there were few Americans there, few French too. I sat at breakfast in the communal "restaurant," really just a basement room with plain wooden tables and chairs. I was reading a French-English dictionary when the only other American in the hotel came up to me; we started talking and decided to travel around together for the day.

She was great company, and we ended up at the Eiffel Tower in the morning, the Louvre in the afternoon, and the Crazy Horse Saloon for an evening cabaret show. As we were leaving the smoke-filled show, a street fight started outside. I didn't notice, but my new friend grabbed me to stop me from getting caught in the fray. Had she not done that, I would have been hurt.

We remained friends for several years. And I have a photo of the two of us in front of the Eiffel Tower that I asked a nearby tourist to take. The experience taught me that strangers can sometimes make the best traveling companions. Of all the friends with whom I've traveled, she was one of the most compatible. We had no expectations of one another. She befriended me and it was a totally positive experience.

Asking for Help (Even if You're a Man)
I recently met a former NFL football player, a large, powerful-

looking man who is well traveled. We were walking together in a large Eastern city after having drinks with mutual acquaintances, and he didn't hesitate to ask for directions. Obviously, he is comfortable with his manliness. Besides, it was late, and it was better to ask than to get lost.

It's a common gender joke that men won't ask for directions. The installation of GPS tracking systems in rental cars is one solution. When traveling, you're in unknown territory, and it's a different kind of query than asking how to get across your hometown. There are, of course, portable GPS tracking systems, but not everyone walks around with one.

This Isn't Trial and Error

If you have unlimited time, if you're staying in a place for a month or more, you can afford the time it takes to discover everything on your own.

However, if time is short, or you're working by day and trying to explore on limited off hours, it pays to ask questions.

When I travel on business, it's often the veteran travelers who know to ask for information on car services and restaurant recommendations. Not asking is more a function of inexperience and self-consciousness than it is a function of gender.

I've traveled with certain female friends who, determined to be independent, refuse to ask for help. I've learned I'm better off by myself so I can ask for assistance rather than having the false comfort of another person with me in a situation where we might both get lost, or in trouble, or are unable to go where we want to go or do what we want to do.

Trips are invariably too short. I like wasting time . . . in a café . . . or a shop . . . or people-watching on the Las Vegas Strip or the *Champs Elysées* in Paris. But I don't like getting lost or missing a beautiful cathedral because I'm with someone hesitant to ask what hours it is open.

That happened to me when I was in Rome with a stubborn female friend—we visited the Colosseum, but when we tried to go to the Roman Forum, it was closed. If we had only asked (or checked a guidebook), we could have rearranged our schedule. Not that there aren't sometimes unexpected or unanticipated closings or other disruptions. But knowing a point of interest is always closed on Mondays or Sunday afternoons or whatever, is valuable information.

> **TIP**
>
> *Asking questions is not a sign of weakness. People like to be helpful, so by giving them the opportunity to dispense advice or directions, you are giving them a gift. It's almost always intriguing to speak with someone who lives wherever your travels take you. Theirs is a unique perspective—something you can't find online or in a guidebook.*

Language is another issue. Even while traveling in the U.S., dialects and colloquialisms can cause communication problems. The only way around those is to ask the person to repeat what they've said. Or to ask someone else to translate.

When you're in a country where they speak another language, at least learn how to say "please" and "thank you," gesture a lot, and smile. A smile is universal. In the stress of the moment, when you're lost in a foreign land, or confused or hungry or tired and cold, you may have to remind yourself to smile. I guarantee that you'll usually be rewarded for it. Not always, but most of the time.

Information from on the Ground

I recently had a flight to Europe out of JFK. I considered taking the shuttle into LaGuardia and then ground transportation between the two airports. I would be doing this on a Sunday afternoon. Unfamiliar with JFK, I asked someone from the airline how long to allow for the transfer. I also asked a friend who lives in New York City for advice.

I was told that if there is an accident, I might be held up on the road for quite a while. There are taxis and shuttle buses, but I decided that my best course of action was to get a domestic flight into JFK, so I didn't need to go from one airport to another. Flight delays are increasingly common, especially at busy airports. I didn't need a ground delay on top of that.

Google.com is a wonderful, ubiquitous search engine. Sometimes though, it's best to solicit opinions of people on the ground before making a decision. Of course, I'm a journalist, so I'm used to asking questions.

Driving Safety

Road trips are fun. My dad took us on drives most Sunday afternoons when my brother and I were growing up. It was a family ritual. At the time, I was a little timid, worrying that we might get lost and worrying that we wouldn't get home in time for me to do my weekend homework, which I invariably left until the last minute.

Yet now I look back on those times with such fondness. I grew up in Baltimore, Maryland, so often Dad would drive us to Pennsylvania. One of my favorite jaunts was to Gettysburg, where we would get out and wander around the immense battlefield, reading the plaques next to the cannons and looking for stray bullets on the ground.

When I take solo car trips now, I listen to a country music radio station whenever I can find one. The country music is fun for me as I sing along whether or not I know all the lyrics, and with nobody along to critique my singing.

Traveling in a car with children or other adults can be distracting. However, other people in the car can keep you alert (unless they're sleeping while you drive).

I sometimes keep long hours; I enjoy staying up late to write far into the night. If I have a trip planned the next day and I have stayed up late, I may take a taxi to the airport. I'll also fly when I'm overtired. But if I'm driving myself to the airport or going on a road trip, I make sure to get enough sleep. Otherwise I postpone my departure until I'm rested.

The dangers of driving while tired can mimic the dangers of driving intoxicated, so it's never a good idea to drive sleepy. I also try to take smaller roads and to stay off major highways whenever possible. It takes longer, but there's more to see and I don't get as tired.

There is a spa in the western U.S. that recommends drivers carry a dry skin brush with them. If the driver feels drowsy, the spa experts recommend that the driver pull into a rest stop and stimulate his or her arms and back with a mini-massage. Getting out of the car to stretch is a good idea too; it stimulates blood circulation and combats stiffness from sitting in the car with your foot on the pedal.

Food on the Road

Eating heavy food can make you groggy, so if you're driving yourself on a car trip, it makes sense to watch what you put into your mouth. I recommend keeping bottled water handy as well as caffeinated coffee or tea or soda. Staying well hydrated will keep you alert and will force you to make frequent stops. Fruit is a better idea than candy or ice cream, so your blood sugar doesn't spike and then crash.

We're a society that often measures success in quantities—how much money, how large a house or boat, how many miles we've traversed. Don't over-goal when driving. Take frequent breaks and stop to eat before you are starving—this will keep you from overeating, which invariably leads to drowsiness and fatigue.

Some of my favorite childhood memories are the times we were driving and stopped to buy fresh peaches or apples at stands on the side of the road. We were wandering in Pennsylvania Dutch country one Sunday and bought the most delicious peaches I have ever tasted in my life. They were huge and juicy and must have been just plucked from the trees. Mom would take a napkin and wipe the dirt off the peaches as best she could, and then hand them over the seat to my brother and me in back. Dad would eat one while he drove and Mom would partake as well.

I have a similar memory of a delicious homemade apple pie we purchased at a roadside stand. Later we stopped at a diner where Mom asked if she could have a knife. They gave her one and as we rode around, she cut slices for each of us and handed them to us. It was one of the best lunches ever!

Stretching . . . and Other Breaks

When you're on a long car trip, it's always a good idea to take breaks. When you stop at a rest stop for gasoline, food, or a restroom, walk around for a few minutes to give your body a break from its sedentary positions in the car. Being confined restricts blood flow, so you want to get all your parts revved up. You can do various stretches standing outside the car. Do not try this while you are driving, and make sure if you stop, you're in a safe, well-lit area away from traffic.

A few recommended stretches:
- Lace your fingers together and put your hands behind your head, pulling your elbows back to stretch the upper back.
- Do a gentle lunge, where the front leg is over the ankle, not the toe, and the back leg is out behind you and straight with

both heels on the ground. Repeat on the other side. These lunges will loosen the hips.
- ✔ Stand up straight with hands on hips and do a gentle side bend to loosen the lower back. Repeat on the other side.

Drinking Water

Water is essential for life. It is present in all our body fluids and tissues, it nourishes our cells and assists us in eliminating waste. Through sweat, water also helps cool our bodies and it cushions and lubricates our joints.

Proper amounts of water are important to keep us hydrated. The trick is to drink the right amount.

A doctor friend recommended that I drink more water when traveling, whether in a car or on a long flight. I took his advice and now I feel better while in transit and when I get wherever I'm going. Trust me, or rather trust my doctor friend—drink more water. I mentioned this earlier, but it is important and it is worth mentioning again.

Buy a bottle of water in the airport terminal before you board, so you have your own before the flight attendants serve drinks, and so you are sure to have extra. Take plenty of water with you in a car or on a train, too.

Safety Guidelines

Remaining safe is a combination of luck, preparation, and staying alert. While not all-inclusive, this list will help:
- ✔ Trust your instincts.
- ✔ Don't announce that you are alone. Tell this to people judiciously. You want to encourage social invitations, but you want to stay safe as well.
- ✔ Avoid deserted places, although crowds can be problematic too. Watch out for any extreme situation.
- ✔ Make sure you leave an itinerary with someone who will check on you if you don't arrive home as planned. If plans change while you're traveling, try to get a message to that person so he or she won't worry and can reach you in an emergency.
- ✔ Ask for help if you need it. This includes if you're lost, sick, or just want to know the best place in town for barbecued ribs.

✓ Carry a flashlight. Even better, carry a light stick, which is lighter and less breakable than a flashlight. During a power outage or on a dark street corner, it can come in handy.

✓ Walk briskly and with a purpose to deter criminals. Don't flash money or jewelry. Carrying keys or an umbrella in your hand will give you a potential weapon. Put keys between your fingers and fist your hand. That way you can use the force of your entire arm and body, rather than just the fingers holding the keys, if you should need to fight off a criminal. By making sure your body language oozes self-confidence, you'll be much less likely to get accosted.

When It Makes Sense to Be Rude

A musician I know used to work in New York City. He was often on his way home at one or two in the morning, wearing a tuxedo. One night a woman stopped and asked him for directions. As he started to answer, her male partner held him up at gunpoint. Luckily, the musician was not harmed, but the incident taught me a lesson.

When I'm out walking, if I can help someone with directions while continuing to keep walking, I will do so. But I never stop. I'd rather be a moving target. This may fly in the face of those willing to share information, but above all, you must be safe.

Being Streetwise

This is going to sound strange, but the best thing that could have happened to me, from a safety standpoint, was being robbed at the Times Square subway station when I was around twenty years old.

I was living and working in New York City that summer between my junior and senior years of college. It was my last day of work. My employer had offered me a full-time job but I was afraid I would never finish college if I stopped and tried to transfer my credits to NYU or Columbia. So I was heading back to the University of Maryland, glad of my decision, but sorry to see my job writing advertising copy at a Madison Avenue agency come to an end.

I was standing on the platform waiting for a train at rush hour, crying softly because I had loved my summer job and knew I would miss it. My arms were full of items from my now former office. My purse was on my shoulder with a flap and no zipper, snap, or Velcro— just a flap.

A man reached into my purse, grabbed my wallet, and pushed me onto an Express train. Luckily, there was a train there and not just empty tracks. The worst part of the experience was the dirty looks I got from other passengers, many of whom had witnessed the robbery. They stood several feet away from me, and there I was, a robbery victim, isolated by the empty space and annoyed stares of the passengers who were giving me a wide berth, even at rush hour on a crowded train.

This robbery turned out to be a gift because it taught me not to be a victim. I travel a lot, but I believe I no longer look like a victim-in-waiting. That day at Times Square, I might as well have worn a sign that said, "rob me, rob me," or played a recording to that effect over and over until someone took me up on the offer.

Staying Alert . . . and Safe

On my one trip to Mexico City, I was somewhat hampered by my negative reaction to the intense smog combined with that city's high altitudes. Lack of sufficient oxygen was slowing me down.

In Chapultepec Park, a wonderful place with the former castle home of the Emperor Maximilian, a fabulous zoo, and much more, I was walking slowly with a travel friend. Three nefarious men started circling us. We went up to a policeman whose English was nonexistent and he began directing us to the zoo. The men laughed, quickly realizing that we were still potential targets. I found an elderly Canadian couple who were happy to stay with us until the men finally gave up and left. I never learned the names of the Canadians or saw them again, but if they happen to read this and remember . . . thank you.

You Made It . . . Now What?

Once your flight gets into a foreign country, here are some basic arrival tips:

- ✓ You'll be expected to go through customs. Have your passport handy, along with a form the flight attendant will give you onboard the flight. You often get the form at the beginning of a flight. After several hours, you'll forget all about it, so as soon as it arrives, fill it out and put it with your passport.
- ✓ Carry some currency for the country you'll be visiting, at least enough for a taxi to your hotel and a meal. There will

probably be a currency exchange booth at the airport but after a long flight while you are carrying your luggage, you'll want to get settled as quickly as possible.

- ✔ Unless you're being met at the airport by a driver, or you want to take public transportation on a subway or bus while dragging your bags, you'll need to find a taxi. Just beware of unofficial cars and drivers; they are unregulated, and you should probably avoid them, especially when you are by yourself. I only had a problem with this on the island of Anguilla in the Caribbean, where the officials were insisting that I take an unmarked taxi. I never did figure out what was going on but it made me wary.

- ✔ Have your valuables secured on your person. No system is foolproof, but zippered pockets are better than open ones, passport wallets on a chain or string around your neck and tucked under your shirt are better than loose passports, and concealed money is better than a wallet bulging in your back pocket.

Short Tours

I like exploring on my own, or with someone else if I'm traveling with another person. But occasionally it makes sense to join up with a tour for a few hours or a few days, and then to go back on your own. I like to do this when there's a specialty tour like one of my previously mentioned favorites—a ghost tour of Charleston, where you wander the streets after dark with a group while a guide tells tales of haunted rooms, houses, and staircases as you pass by those places. On my "to do" list is a tour tracking clues from *The Da Vinci Code* in cities like London, Paris, Edinburgh, and Milan.

It also makes sense to take a brief familiarization tour if you're in another country and want to visit a place in the countryside without renting a car. A tour simplifies the excursion by eliminating the need to deal with the difficulties of international licenses, insurance, rental car fees, rules of the road, and unfamiliar routes.

It is generally easy to get around cities using public transport. However, a short tour of a major city will familiarize you with the main points of interest. This is useful if it's your first visit, or if it's been a while since you were last there.

In many countries though, a train schedule and an adventurous spirit are all you need because train service is often more prevalent and more accessible than here in the States. A good example would be if you were in Paris and wanted to take a day trip to Versailles. You can catch a train and do it on your own. Or you can take a day tour by bus.

Another option is to contact a tourist board or hotel concierge

IT'S ALL IN THE NUMBERS

Temperature conversions:
- From Fahrenheit (F) to Celsius [Centrigrade] (C), subtract 32, multiply by 5, and divide by 9.
- From Celsius to Fahrenheit, multiply by 9, divide by 5, and add 32.
- If you are without a calculator or dislike math, you can get an approximation if you subtract 30 going from Fahrenheit and divide by 2. Reversing it from Celsius, multiply by 2 and add 30.
- Note that water freezes at 32 degrees F and zero degrees C.

Distance conversions:
- One kilometer (km) is equal to 0.621 mile.
- One mile is equivalent to 1.609 kilometers.

Weight conversions:
- One gram equals 0.03527 ounce.
- One ounce is equivalent to 28.35 grams.
- One kilogram is equal to 2.2046 pounds.

Liquid conversions:
- One gallon equals 3.785 liters.
- One liter is equivalent to 0.264 gallon.

Currency conversions:
- Use google.com or another search engine to obtain appropriate currency information.

wherever you're going and arrange for a car service to provide an English-speaking driver to chauffeur you around.

Trust Your Instincts

When I went on a short cruise, I was concerned when they spent the entire safety drill asking how we were enjoying the ship rather than telling us what to do or where to go in an emergency. Having never before been on a cruise, I asked several employees of the cruise line if there were extra life jackets somewhere in case we were unable, due to fire or flood, to get back to our staterooms for our life jackets. I was told not to worry; and I was told they did not know. One person from the cruise line even made fun of me for worrying too much.

As it turned out, a month later, there was a problem with that same ship turning too suddenly. Flooding occurred on the top decks when the ship tilted, and several people were injured. Something didn't seem right to me—safety-wise—when I was out in the Atlantic Ocean on that ship. A month later I was proven right.

On the night of their accident, the cruise ship had intended to show the movie *Titanic*. Luckily, passenger injuries were apparently not severe. But what were they thinking? Planning to show *Titanic* on a cruise would be like showing an airport disaster flick on a flight. A light comedy would be a better choice.

Hot Air Balloon

On a visit to Alsace in France, I agreed to take a hot air balloon ride from a field in the countryside. The balloon had holes in it. When I asked about the holes before we went up, I was told not to worry, that they didn't matter. Once we were up about a mile above the earth, the man in charge of the balloon lit a cigarette while he stood next to, and operated, the propane gas tank.

"Is that a good idea—to smoke?" I asked, not wanting to anger him in this little crowded basket with no safe way down without him.

"I love to smoke, so yes, of course it's a good idea," was his answer. Except for my concern over the holes and potential sparks, I found the balloon ride fairly interesting on the way up, but when we hovered for a long time in the sky, I was ready to come down. No one warned me to brace for the eventual rough landing either, so I was jolted more roughly than I liked.

Recently, there were some deaths from falls and fire in a few hot air balloon accidents. I'm glad I went up in the balloon when I did so I know what it's like. However, I don't plan to ever repeat the experience. At a party recently, we started talking about hot air balloons, and a business associate told me he had a similar experience. Even though the ride had been his idea during a family vacation, he was fearful like me and would not do it again. "But my kids will probably want to go again," he said.

Staying Healthy

If possible, make sure that you are well rested while traveling. It's impossible to avoid people with coughs or other signs of illness, so if you're rested you have a better chance to fight off the germs. If I'm seated next to someone who's sick on a plane, I'm kind of stuck. But if I'm in a store or restaurant, I'll try to reposition myself without getting nutty about it.

I have a theory that is not necessarily supported by scientific evidence but only by my experience, that when we travel to different places we expose ourselves to unfamiliar germs. This does not have to be just when we travel to the jungle or other undeveloped areas.

On my first trip to Paris, I acquired a miserable cold that took me two months to shake once I came home. I've not gotten sick in Paris since. Perhaps I've built up antibodies to Parisian germs.

I don't mean in any way to instill fear, just caution. After all, the reality is that we are in a global society and much of this stuff travels to us anyway.

I used to worry about getting sick from shaking someone's hand. Then a friend told me, "You could drink bad water, eat food with bugs from a good restaurant, eat contaminated food from a street vendor, sleep in a bed that has germs and isn't clean, or be exposed to coughing on a plane, train, or bus. Why worry about just shaking hands?" I laughed, and I haven't worried about that since.

Smoothing the Way

A large reason for travel, especially solo, is getting to know how people live in other places, soaking up the culture and ambiance, trying new foods and learning different flavors, shopping, touring, absorbing the history of a place and its people. You can't do this the same way through books or videos, talking with people who have been there, or searching the Internet.

However, a little research goes a long way. It will never be what you expected, but it's nice to avoid total culture shock. If you have an idea of the history of a place, or the pirate battles, or ancient civilizations that thrived in the area, you will appreciate the journey infinitely more. And you will be less likely to offend those you meet along the way, since you'll have a better appreciation for the place where they reside, as well as for their way of life.

Stuff Happens

We sometimes make a bad decision, or we make a good decision that goes bad. Therefore, it is smart to know where the U.S. embassy is located if you're an American, or another embassy if you're from a different country. It is a good idea to have extra money too, or to have access to money through a credit card or someone back home willing to wire money to you.

Money talks. In an emergency, cash is king. You don't want to carry too much, but you need to have some. It can buy bottled water in a crisis, or a ride to safety. It gives you flexibility and provides options. It certainly never hurts.

Keep cash handy in varying denominations of the local currency, so you don't have to hand over $100 for a bottle of water when $10 would do.

It's also a good idea to keep an eye on the U.S. State Department website for travel warnings (travel.state.gov). The website advises Americans as to which countries are judged unsafe for travel. You should also stay current by following news and weather conditions for places where you are headed or have already arrived.

Chapter 6

FOLLOWING YOUR PASSIONS

A friend once told me, "Nine out of ten times, living out your fantasies will be disappointing—but that tenth time—watch out." That has certainly proven true of many things—when they are great, they are truly great. When it comes to travel though, the percentages are reversed, and nine out of ten times I am entranced. As a result, the more I travel, the more I want to go again. Not to the same place. Not to do the same thing, though sometimes that is the case.

Most often, my favorite place is the next place I am going—preferably someplace I've never been before.

The Power of Movement

Staying still is not an option. Just as we run and jog and lift weights to stay physically fit, some of us need to go places and move around to stay emotionally and mentally charged.

From armchair travelers to true wanderers and everything in between, we are interested in traversing land, sea, air, even space.

Self-propelled movement includes walking, swimming, skydiving, hiking, running, jumping, skipping, snowshoeing, snow skiing, snow boarding, hang gliding, water-skiing, scuba diving, and snorkeling—all modes of moving by your own volition, and there's nothing like it. Modes of transport can help . . . by car, rail, air, hot air balloon, dog sled, tram, zip-line, kayak, helicopter, dirt bike, motorcycle, and moped—transportation can help you get where you're going. The idea is to keep moving until you find a place you want to be.

For Love of the Railroad

When I was a little girl growing up in Baltimore, my dad worked as a structural engineer for the B & O Railroad where he designed bridges and buildings. I told this to someone recently who commented that he thought the B & O Railroad was just a made-up stop on the Monopoly board. Well, it is a stop on that board game, but it was also one of the major East Coast railroads in the heyday of the railroads. B & O stood for the Baltimore and Ohio Railroad; and it later merged with the C & O, or Chesapeake and Ohio Railroad. One of the perks my dad got from his job was travel on the trains. When I was about six and my brother was four, my family and I took a train from Baltimore's Pennsylvania Station (much smaller than the one in New York City) to Washington, DC's Union Station. There we visited the Capitol building and looked at the Washington Monument. We also ate lunch and came back the same day on a later train.

That was all it took for me to fall in love with rail travel. Now, when I take a train ride either in this country or in other countries where train travel is often more luxurious and efficient, I am always charmed. The lulling and swaying of the train on the tracks appeals to me.

For those traveling solo, you don't need a companion on a train. It's a thought-provoking means of travel, less stressful than air flight and with more room.

With train travel, you have the benefit of being able to move about the train car, or even to cross into another car. You get to see the scenery—mountains and rivers and marinas, sometimes slums in urban areas, as well as fields—and to cross railroad bridges, some of which my dad may have worked on.

For those traveling solo, you don't need a companion on a train. It's a thought-provoking means of travel, less stressful than air flight and with more room. You can walk around and observe the scenery and the other passengers. It is easier in some ways than driving a car, and you can usually plan it on the spur of the moment unless you want to take a unique trip on a train like the legendary Orient-Express or the Canadian transcontinental train.

I like train stations too. This is partially due to my love of the railroads. But who would not get a thrill seeing Grand Central Station in New York? If nothing else, one is moved by the charm of seeing where so many films have taken place. Liverpool Street Station in London and Milan's central train station are equally fascinating; it's great fun to imagine the possible destinations of all the people rushing around.

I haven't been to that many train stations, but the ones I have visited left a strong impression. On my to-do list, wherever I go, is to take a train if it makes sense where I'm going.

The Allure of Water

We're all attracted to different places and things. However, it is the passion that is important, not the particular interest.

Whatever your quest, as long as it does no harm to you or others, I encourage you to pursue it. If you love trains, there's a train museum you should visit, or a trip you should take by rail.

If you love the ocean, visit an island, take a cruise, or go on a deep-sea fishing jaunt.

I am drawn to bodies of water as if they were magnets. Perhaps because we are all made up mostly of water, there is an allure, a fascination to it. Perhaps because my mom's idea of a summer vacation was invariably to take us to the beach, I grew up believing the ocean to be "special." To me, large bodies of water impart positive karma.

I love Chicago, in large part because the omnipresent Lake Michigan holds a fascination for me. Give me a hotel room with a view that overlooks Lake Michigan, and I'm delighted.

Waking up to a view of water almost anywhere, actually moves me to ecstasy. This connection to water is not mine alone. After all, the lure of water has attracted people for centuries. This is why spas were created, starting with the mineral baths in ancient Greece, followed by the baths that the Romans built later throughout their Empire.

Water has meant sustenance and transportation to civilizations throughout the world. It defines many places and never fails to intrigue if you let yourself be captivated by its powerful aura.

A Diametric Opposite

I love deserts too. I truly believe this is because the watering holes and oases around which we congregate in the desert—the Mecca of Las Vegas, for instance, or resorts with hot springs—evolved around places that have life-supporting water.

Las Vegas proponents and detractors all debate the reasons so many people flock there from throughout the U.S. and the rest of the world. In Vegas, there's gambling, of course, as well as fine food,

> **TIP**
>
> *If you find yourself in London, it's well worth a day's excursion by train to and from the city of Bath in southwest England. The train ride is less than two hours each way. Bath was initially inhabited by the Romans, who took advantage of the natural thermal springs found there. Later the city became popular with the British aristocracy.*
>
> *Other water-related opportunities include visits to the Thames River in London with its many majestic bridges, or the Seine in Paris also with its many bridges, the Potomac in Washington, DC, the Mediterranean Sea, the vast oceans, and many, many lakes—there are a myriad of fabulous bodies of water to see, just about everywhere on this earth of ours.*
>
> *If you're in St. Louis or New Orleans, there's the mighty Mississippi, in Egypt the Nile, and in New Hampshire, Lake Winnipesaukee. I won't list them all. But next time you're somewhere fascinated by a body of water, know that you're not alone.*

superb spas, elegant resorts, and provocative shows. There is an ever-changing cacophony of sensual triggers, from bells and whistles to neon and fluorescent lights. All these are present in abundance in Las Vegas, along with sensuous, provocative, flowing water—yes water, even here in the desert—in pools and man-made lakes and canals, in fish tanks, showers, and drinks.

Las Vegas is an oasis in the desert that beckons travelers as if on a pilgrimage, while quenching many thirsts and many desires.

Las Vegas is one of my favorite destinations because the city is surrounded by desert, and seductive water is a dominant theme. Spokespersons for the various resorts don't like to talk about the water. After all, there is a limited supply and huge amounts of development have put a strain on resources. But they do recycle water at many of the resorts.

Las Vegas' main attraction has always been water, even way back. Prehistoric southern Nevada was a virtual marsh that receded over time, with water trapped underground. When it sporadically surfaced in the Las Vegas Valley, an oasis was created, hidden from discovery by the surrounding Mojave Desert.

Native Americans were the only ones who knew about the oasis until 1829. By 1890, railroad developers were paying attention, and by 1937, with the taming of the Colorado River at the Hoover Dam, Las Vegas' place on the map was cemented.

Authorities are working to expand water capacity to meet anticipated and growing demands. After all, this *is* the desert, and there is always the possibility of running out of water.

Next time you visit Las Vegas, it may not just be to play blackjack or poker. It might be to revel in a pool or to drink a cool drink beside a fountain.

On Spirituality—Yours or Others

Churches, cathedrals, synagogues, the Wailing Wall, mosques, monasteries, and the Vatican—organized religion has left many places for us to visit spirituality, our own and others.

Then there is the draw of nature. Driving along the California coastline, one is awed by the potentiality of a greater being who has created such beauty, such drama. On the big island of Hawaii, the moonscape of black lava fields is juxtaposed against the Pacific Ocean to offer more dramatic evidence.

On sacred lands of Native Americans, one might feel an otherworldliness. When I was at Tamaya, in New Mexico, I definitely felt a spirituality in the very air and on the earth as I stood outside and looked at what was, at that point, a very narrow Rio Grande River. The land at Tamaya is part of a reservation, and its spirituality was unmistakable to me.

On this earth, there is much evidence of beauty and grandeur, many places where nature and spirituality merge. I challenge you to find your own.

Labyrinths

On the coast of Maine, I walked a circular labyrinth of stones, more awed by the ocean crashing against the cliff beside me than by the act of walking around the circle. But I did walk the labyrinth looking for something inside myself—in case the labyrinth triggered a deeper awareness or understanding. The experience was peaceful at least, and it triggered a desire for me to walk other labyrinths in other places.

Many labyrinths are patterned after a famous circular one that dates back to the thirteenth century at the Chartres Cathedral in France. What I particularly like about labyrinths is that there are supposedly no right or wrong ways to walk one, because a labyrinth is not a maze or a puzzle with dead ends. Although you have your eyes open and are looking where you are walking, the focus is internal since the path is in full view and thus is not difficult to traverse.

As a result, the walker can concentrate on his or her individual, internal journey. That parallels my approach to travel in general— that you wind in and out of places and people's lives, with the important journey the one you are taking for yourself.

Visiting Historic Cemeteries

As a kid on my family's road trip through New England, my father stopped at a few historic cemeteries. Instead of being morbid, I found it interesting to see where the figures of American history were laid to rest. I was with my family, this was fun, no one particularly close to me had died yet in my young life, and there was historical context.

So began what has become an occasional interest in historic cemeteries. Unfortunately, I have since lost several people who were extremely close to me. Going to the cemeteries where people I love are buried is different than going to Arlington National Cemetery and seeing the Kennedy graves, to which I have no personal attachment. Similarly, many admirers visit Elvis' grave at Graceland.

Less prominent cemeteries can be interesting too. I was traveling through part of Wisconsin with a longtime friend from high school when we passed a lone cemetery in a rather rural area. I wanted to stop and look around, but she thought I was being morbid. I tried to explain, but she wasn't really listening. I left her in the rental car for a few minutes as I wandered around the cemetery alone.

I didn't know anyone, either personally or historically, who was buried there. But since the cemetery was in a rural area, this was *the* area cemetery. Interestingly, there were several religions represented together, which is unusual. Tombstones are always interesting, as they tell a bit of history about those who are buried beneath.

This interest in cemeteries is no different from the fascination that many have with Egyptian burial practices, along with discoveries from the ancient tombs and pyramids.

Sports, Sports, and More Sports

In talking with a businessman I met in California, he told me about his preference for travel when it's not for business. "I like going to Hilton Head, South Carolina, to play golf," he told me. "I'm always changing something with my game. Anywhere I can play is a good place—I don't have a favorite. Just so it's a nice course, nice scenery. Mostly it depends on how well I'm playing. If I'm playing well, it's a great place. My problem is that I don't play enough.

"I used to travel and take my clubs because I like to play with my own clubs—it's like wearing your own shoes, you don't have to readjust. It's really more psychological than anything else."

For me, personally, I watched Tiger Woods on television playing a course at Pebble Beach. Even through the TV, I fell in love with the beauty of the place as well as the icon's mastery of the sport. So I decided to learn how to play.

It was not so easy to trade my afternoon tea parties for "tee parties." I've since taken lessons in Arizona, Florida, and Pennsylvania. I also spent an afternoon inside a Virginia golf club learning about the etiquette of the game, frustrated because all I wanted to do was go outside and whack the balls. It didn't happen that day. I still think it's a beautiful sport. I'm just haunted by the fact that what looks so easy is actually rather difficult.

Creating New Passions

I used to have a lot of friends who liked downhill skiing. They'd go in groups to various mountains in different states. I realized that I never got invited along.

I asked once why I was never included. "You don't ski," was the answer. Duh.

So I decided to learn. I took myself out to Aspen, Colorado, for a week of lessons and skiing. I've never been so tired in all my life; I virtually fell into bed each night, usually without dinner, for I was using muscles that I didn't know I had for hours each day.

It was great. Skiing down the mountain for the first time, with trees whizzing by me, I thought that if I stopped to think, I would kill myself. So I just went with the moment. It was utterly exhilarating.

The following year, I joined a ski club that had a planned trip to Lake Tahoe with about 100 of its members; I thought that would be a great next step. As the trip got closer, someone in charge at the club decided that Aspen would be a better destination, so they switched the trip there. Of all the ski resorts in the U.S. and elsewhere, I had only ever skied in Aspen and I wanted a new experience. I went ahead and booked a room at the Tahoe hotel where the club had originally planned to go. Once again I was skiing and traveling solo.

Not really, of course. Tahoe in the wintertime is crazy busy, and the Texas Ski Club was in town. Besides having men fighting to take me out, I was showered with gifts and even a marriage proposal. I was actually having trouble spending time by myself. No one would leave me alone!

The good thing about Tahoe—I could take a day off when my muscles were tired, and there was plenty to do besides skiing. I even won a jackpot on a slot machine. Of course, big gambler that I am, I was only playing a nickel slot machine. The machine said I won 1,600. Great, I thought—$1,600! But my winnings were 1,600 nickels, the equivalent of $80. Still, it was fun, and I remember how dirty my hands got from two hours of handling nickels.

After that second ski trip, my friends started inviting me along on their group trips. But I'll tell you a secret—I always had a better time when I went on my own. People strike up friendships in the lift line or at the après ski bar. I like my friends, of course. But they're hardcore skiers and I'm more of a dabbler.

I prefer skiing for a half day and playing the rest of the time. On my own, there were no pulls on my time, unless they were of my own making. It's not like I was really alone—there were thousands of fellow revelers, many of whom also wanted to do more than just ski (not that there's anything wrong with focusing on the skiing if you love it that much).

Day Trip to Squaw Valley

This was the best skiing ever, for me at least. From Tahoe, I took a bus up to the former Olympic site in Squaw Valley for the day. It was snowing, a quiet, steady snow. The intermediate trail was rather wide, so I could maneuver it with my beginner level skills. I took a tram up the mountain. Since lifts scare me a little, the tram ride was great, though in the middle of a snowstorm, it was swaying a bit more than I liked.

Once on the mountain in the steady snow, the beauty and quiet were overwhelmingly charming. I loved every minute of it. And I did it all on my own. This was quite a memorable experience for me, a relative non-skier, to accomplish. At nighttime, the bus took me back to Tahoe, so I didn't need to make any special arrangements or accommodations.

Baseball Stadiums

It's fun to have specific interests. I used to travel with a particular boyfriend I dated for a while; he loved baseball, so wherever we went, we'd get tickets and catch a game. I do this now, even when I'm by myself. I adore visiting all the stadiums.

Recently I attended a Nationals game, and I met some men who had traveled from Boston to Washington, DC, to catch the game. They had already seen the Orioles play at Baltimore's Camden Yards. I was able to chat with them about Fenway, Wrigley, Yankee, and Shea—even the stadium in downtown Buffalo where the AAA Bisons play. I've been to games in Houston and St. Louis too. I can't necessarily speak about the players or team stats, but I know about the best seats and food, and the differences in ambiance—that's what intrigues me.

Sports events are great venues for solo travelers. Surrounded by thousands of people, the excitement is pervasive.

If it's basketball or tennis, I'm busy watching the game or match. But with baseball, it's the color that gets to me. Sports events are great venues for solo travelers. Surrounded by thousands of people, the excitement is pervasive.

Central Park

One of my dearest friends tells me that her favorite pastime in New York City is to walk and jog in Central Park. When I asked why, she told me that it's vibrant and fun.

"I even saw Sting there," she told me. "He shook his head at me, as if to say, 'Yes, I am who you think I am.' It was exciting."

It's best to go running or walking in Central Park, or any other park anywhere in the world, during daylight for safety reasons. Of course, you'll see more during the day too.

I was amazed this year when I went walking in Central Park with someone who used to live in New York. We ran into several of his friends. In such a big city, in such a large park, there was still the feeling of a real hometown.

Shopping—A "Sin"tillating Pastime

At a business conference, a woman I know told me of a study that shows women prefer shopping to just about anything, including sex. I wouldn't go that far, and I've known men who like to shop too. I'm also sure that many men and women would prefer sex. That aside, when traveling, the allure of the shops and street merchants is more than most people can resist.

There are malls just about everywhere, as well as extravagant, high-end shops in places such as Chicago's Michigan Avenue, New York City's Fifth Avenue, or Rodeo Drive in Beverly Hills. Then, there is nothing like the silver jewelry in Taxco, Mexico, or the hand-painted silk scarves on the *Rue de Rivoli* in Paris. I bought a fabulous storyteller doll from its Native American artist at the Palace of the Governors in Santa Fe, and it sits in a prominent place on my bookshelves, reminding me every day that the art of storytelling does not reside in only writers like me.

Then there are the mistakes I've made shopping, like the chess board and pieces made of quartzite and onyx that I bargained for in Mexico City long ago. Heavy as all get out, I lugged it home in my carry-on, afraid that it would be damaged in my checked luggage. To this day, the board and the pieces sit in the bottom of my closet, taking up room. While I know how to play chess, I've never used this particular chess set. I keep figuring that some day I'll have a bigger house with room to put it out.

I have a handmade lace pillow that I bought on the island of Burano, a neighbor of Murano. Both islands are short boat rides away from Venice, Italy. Burano is the lesser known island where elderly women sit and make handmade lace, just as the residents of their nearby island make the classic Murano glass on the bigger, more commercial island next door. The lace pillow was a good purchase; I only wish I'd bought more than one.

In Venice, I bought one of the masks for which they are famous due to their preoccupation with Carnival. I also bought two exquisite hand-painted watercolors of clowns—simple, elegant little paintings. One is framed on my wall, the other securely tucked away to be brought out around the time I rescue the chess set from obscurity.

In Ireland, I escaped from the group with which I was traveling for one glorious day on my own in Dublin. Wandering around Dublin was easy for me. At that point, I was also in need of alone time. Shopping seemed a good idea, and my niece had asked me for a claddagh ring, in which a heart shape is created by the outline of two hands.

I spent a while going from jewelry shop to jewelry shop—one of my favorite indulgences. I found a ring for my niece, and I had a glorious time. Out on my own, I got a chance to really interact with the Irish shopkeepers, to understand a little about how proud they are of their small shops, about the ebb and flow of business, and their dependence on tourists.

In Florence, I love to window shop on the *Ponte Vecchio*. There's also a fabulous leather shop on a street nearby where I discovered wonderful leather boxes. You can find leather boxes in many stores in that city, but these particular boxes are exquisite. I bought several for gifts and kept one for myself. I also bought myself two small Limoges enamel boxes in France, for I love little boxes.

I know a woman who has an international Pez collection. People she knows buy them for her from all over the world. It doesn't matter what you collect—postcards or matchbooks, photos or works by local artists, clothing or jewelry or chess sets—it's just good to have something you like to accumulate.

Or you can buy different things in different places—no two with any similarity other than that you chose them all. You can be the common denominator, the passion behind the purchase. Wherever you go, the things you buy will remind you of your trip and bring you happy, if wistful, memories of your time in a special place.

Off to the Races

It's fun to go somewhere you haven't planned when an opportunity arises and you take it. Often, when a trip happens quickly or unexpectedly, you can have a really good time. You have no expectations, mostly because you haven't had time to develop any, and therefore everything that happens is a treat. It's also great fun to have a list of places and things you want to do sometime in the future. One of mine is attending the Kentucky Derby.

What I want is to see the horse race of all races at least once, in person—which will take me to Louisville, Kentucky, hopefully sometime soon.

I'm from Baltimore and I've been to the Preakness several times. Watching thoroughbred racing runs in my family, on my paternal side. My dad and I used to watch the Triple Crown races together on television when he was alive. My cousin tells me that my grandfather liked to go to the races too. I suspect he took my dad with him, though I never asked.

Whenever someone tells me they've been to the Kentucky Derby, I quiz them on what it's like. This happened recently, when a business associate told me, "It's visual overload—the Derby, the pageantry, every woman beautiful on Derby day. The women are in their hats and the men are in their ties. Oh, yeah, there are horses too. And people-watching. There's chaos and bedlam on the infield and the Kentucky gentry in the stands."

She went on to tell me that there are lots of parties to benefit charities. "But the best part is absorbing the atmosphere, the excitement, the hats, and the men in their brightly colored ties and sport coats."

She warned me that the hotels often have a three-night minimum at Derby time and that the rates are higher than usual. "They can get away with it, so the entire experience is expensive—beyond the tickets. And you need to have a source for tickets."

As to the etiquette of the event, "If you're a woman, you can go without a hat. They will let you in the gate, but they frown." I can hardly wait.

Card Please

I recently went to Austin, Texas, and learned how to play Texas Hold 'Em—a popular type of poker. In the past, when I've been anywhere there's a casino, I've played blackjack.

Next time I go to a casino, I plan to try poker—although with just a small amount of money. I'm willing to gamble the equivalent of the cost for dinner and a show; thus my gambling budget—whether it's for blackjack or poker—is only an entertainment expense. My goal is to play for at least an hour before I lose my stake. I never add to the stake once I'm at the table. I find it's easier to walk away when I've predetermined the amount I'm willing to spend for my entertainment. I have no illusions about my gambling personality. As long as I'm playing with the house's money, I'll generally stay. But even then, if I'm up and I see the trend is changing, I'm willing to walk away. Because of this, I figure that cards are an okay hobby for me. I'll never be a big winner, but I won't lose much either. And I love the excitement of the activity, the people watching, and the entertainers—either singers or comedians—who are often nearby.

Flop, Turn, River
Participating in a poker tournament or going to a casino to play poker is something that would be easy to do by yourself. It's social, it's playful, and you'll probably enjoy yourself. Just don't gamble more than you can afford to lose, and it will be a fun time.

For those non-poker players reading this, "flop," "turn," and "river" are terms from Texas Hold 'Em. In Austin, I was taught the basics and told to watch televised tournaments to better learn the game and the strategies employed by top players. It's amazing to me how much fun it is to watch these poker tournaments on television. I'd rather be in an actual casino, but until I can get to one, this is a great interim measure.

Pick Your Own Passion
I used to know someone who loved covered bridges. She traveled all around the country looking for, and at, whatever bridges she could find. That was her passion.

I've met other people who love to fish, or bird-watch, or collect shot glasses from different places.

I have friends who love the movies; they travel to the Sundance Film Festival every year without fail.

I know people more timid than I am and some who are more daring. Some of my friends go snowboarding in the winter and others sit on the beach reading every summer. I have my own personal passions, yet I'm always willing to consider adding new ones. I know I won't go skydiving, but I'd be willing to try water-skiing.

It doesn't matter what your interests or desires happen to be, just that you pursue them. And it's important that you're open to going places and doing things. We are all different, each and every one of us. What we have in common is the fact of our passions, not their origins.

Chapter 7
PLANNING FOR THE UNEXPECTED

The more you venture out of your comfort zone and the further you travel from home, the more unfamiliar everything will seem. Thinking ahead, doing research online, and talking with other travelers can help you anticipate what might happen. But unless you're omniscient, and none of us are, you'll need to count on your self-confidence and skills to get you through. Although it may be hard to distinguish between fear of the unknown and excitement, assume it's mostly excitement and enjoy the thrills of your adventure.

From Snowstorms to Sunburn

I went on a trip to Maryland's Eastern Shore with a friend. It was spring, so I didn't expect the weather to play a role in our driving there and back. However, once there, we learned that the Bay Bridge, which spans the Chesapeake Bay, was closed due to the dangers from high winds—not something we could anticipate, as it is rather unusual.

My friend panicked; she wanted to get back to work. I never plan a trip without leaving a day or two between when I return and when I absolutely positively must be somewhere or do something. Pet care, child care, jury duty, dinner at the White House, an appearance on national television—whatever you have planned, build in some time for delay—just in case.

Maine During a Nor'easter

I went to a resort on the Maine coast for a few days off-season. It was charming and just what I needed—time alone in a beautiful if somewhat remote location to think and plan the next chapter of my life. To get to the resort, I had to take a coastal road with the Atlantic Ocean just a few feet on one side and a canal of some sort on the other. The road was like a narrow low bridge, so I carefully maneuvered my rental car, glad I was arriving during the day.

A few days later, a nor'easter hit; the wind howled and the rain poured down. I was comfortably ensconced inside, where I was being well fed in the restaurant and cared for in the spa. Waves crashed against the shore. It was fun to look outside where the elements were angry, while inside we had electricity and the comforts of attentive service provided by a well-run resort.

The weather started to clear the day I was scheduled to leave. I asked about travel conditions and learned that the road might be washed out. "If it is, just back up your car," I was told. This made me extremely nervous, and I debated with myself, and anyone who would listen, as to whether or not I should stay put or chance the two-hour drive to Manchester, New Hampshire, and the airport.

A woman overheard and came over to say, "If I were you, I'd wait. I used to live here in Maine, and they're just tough here. You're not being overly-cautious." I stayed the extra day and was glad I did because the next day I got lost twice on my way to the highway. Had the roads been washed out, it would have added stress to what had been an otherwise relaxing holiday.

I was also having a good time, and I didn't mind having an extra day of pampering. I paid a small change fee to the airline and added an extra day onto my rental car agreement. If possible, it's always a good idea to have extra money in your budget to cover schedule changes.

Not What You Thought Would Happen

Flying is such a large part of travel, that it's good to be prepared for change—in the weather, in the type of plane you'll be on (which can alter your seat assignment), in security measures (which may affect what you can pack or carry onboard), delayed ground transportation, overbooking, and other contingencies.

On a recent trip to Ireland, I was flying from Boston to Shannon, Ireland, and then back from Dublin through Chicago. My connecting flights were less than optimal. On the way out, I had a layover of six hours in Boston, and on the way back, only about a half hour to clear customs in Chicago and board my domestic flight back home. Those two extremes on the same trip taught me a lesson—to try to avoid a too tight layover rush, but not to waste more time in an airport than necessary.

In anticipation of that six-hour layover in Boston, I informally polled a few friends to find out how they would entertain themselves during such a long layover. Here's what they told me:

- ✔ I'd read a book.
- ✔ I'd leave the airport and get transportation into Boston.
- ✔ I'd arrange a different flight; I would never have that long a layover.
- ✔ I'd work on my computer and listen to my iPod.
- ✔ I'd shop.
- ✔ I'd sleep.

One friend wisely advised me to get the DVD for Steven Spielberg's film *The Terminal* with Tom Hanks and Catherine Zeta-Jones. That film gives a whole new meaning to waiting around in an airport. Later, when I was planning a trip from New York's JFK to London, I made sure I had a reasonable two-hour layover. During that layover at JFK, the supposed setting for Spielberg's film, I had to change terminals because I was changing airline carriers. Someone told me to take the AirTrain, which is a light-rail system that links to the subway but also circles the airport and stops at the different terminals. Once found, it was a breeze. But I had never flown into or out of JFK before so I was confused and couldn't, at first, follow the signage to the AirTrain.

I tried asking several people about AirTrain, but the people I asked appeared not to understand English. I started to empathize with Tom Hanks' character in the movie.

Getting Around an Airport

It makes sense to go online and check out an unfamiliar airport before you spend any time in one, especially if it is a large airport. If you do advance research, it will be more readily understandable that "Skylink" is the high-speed train at Dallas Fort Worth International Airport (DFW), for instance, and that the Wiki Wiki is the shuttle service at Honolulu International Airport—invaluable for getting around between the terminals. And so on.

If you've been to an airport before, or it is relatively small, this probably isn't necessary. Just don't count on much help once you're on the ground at a large airport.

I was at Washington Dulles Airport recently and asked for directions. I was met with blank stares and given incorrect information. I'd been to the airport before, but airports evolve over time. Between the changes, the fact I that normally don't drive and park there, and confusing signage, a little advance knowledge would have made the process more user-friendly.

Remember that each airport is different, but so are their websites. Finding the Wiki Wiki in Honolulu was easy at the airport because there were employees directing us when we disembarked; finding it on the website was a bit trickier. I had to ask a few times before I could figure out Dallas' Skylink at DFW. Had I gone online in advance of visiting Dallas, the website makes it pretty clear.

When Traveling Is a Marathon

I heard a story about a woman who, with several of her friends, planned a trip to run the Anchorage, Alaska, marathon.

As happens to many of us at some time, one by one, this woman's friends backed out. They no doubt each had a reason, and maybe all the excuses were good ones. Determined to go anyway, this woman flew to Alaska by herself, rented a car, ran the marathon, and while sitting in a bar afterward, ran into people she knew from back home on the East Coast.

Even if you don't plan on traveling solo, stuff happens to cause traveling companions to bail out of a planned trip.

This woman happened to be someone who is willing to get on a plane at the drop of a hat. But she proves a good point. Even if you don't plan on traveling solo, stuff happens to cause traveling companions to bail out of a planned trip.

I did this myself to a good friend years ago. She and I had planned to travel to Europe together. I was young and this was to be my first trip to Europe. I wanted to map out a loose agenda and wing it, which tends to me my style. My friend wanted to sign up with a tour group and have everything organized for us. If we went her way, we would wake in Paris on Monday, and by Tuesday, we would be in Belgium. The trip she chose for us cost thousands of dollars—a king's ransom for me at the time.

So, for my first trip to Europe, I would be spending more than I could afford and traveling in a way that I already knew didn't suit me. My friend didn't want to do it my way, and although we tried to find a compromise, we couldn't.

I opted to stay home and she went anyway. To her credit, this never affected our friendship. I remember thinking that I wouldn't have been too happy with her if the roles had been reversed. As I write this, I realize that she chose to go alone rather than compromise what she wanted, since I would have taken the trip if it had been devised differently.

My friend cheerfully shared her photos and her experiences with me upon her return. Later, she was happy for me when I finally made it to Europe myself, and she even gave me tips on what to do before I went. She was just a good soul and a true friend; her husband has told me that she saw me as, "a particularly special friend."

In our way, my friend and I shared travel stories, if not the travel itself. It is this way for many of us with our busy lives and varying schedules. To the woman who ran the Anchorage marathon without her friends, good for her.

I decided I would never plan a trip that I wouldn't or couldn't take by myself if circumstances changed and my planned traveling companion either backed out, or else I decided that I'd be better off on my own.

A Broken Seat Belt . . . Right

On a flight to California, I had a layover in Phoenix during which time we switched to a smaller plane. In the waiting area, I overheard the pilot say that it was his first time flying this particular plane. Then I overheard the flight attendant say that it was her first time too. Great, I thought. At least there was a second pilot, and I hoped he had more experience.

As it turned out, the flight was delayed for an hour because the flight attendant said her seat belt was broken. I immediately guessed that she just didn't know how to operate it from her jump seat.

Both pilots came out to try to fix the seat belt, and they radioed to a repair crew. When it was finally determined that the flight attendant just didn't know how the seat belt worked, we had to wait for clearance from a government inspector.

Eventually, we arrived safely and without further incident, which is the important part. However, we were on a little plane with just the one flight attendant. After takeoff, she cried for a while, and then she took so long serving drinks that she ran out of time and never got to most of us.

The funny part of this story is that the flight attendant didn't even bother trying to use the seat belt upon landing. I imagine she's since found a new career.

Luckily, I wasn't in a hurry that day so the delay was merely amusing. It's always a good idea to leave extra time in your schedule . . . just in case.

Trusting Yourself

You can never really know what's going to happen, no matter how well you plan. That's the source of the adrenaline rush. That's also the source of the fear. But like a scary movie, travel is exciting. You prepare to "wing it," to talk to strangers, to cross the street after looking both ways (even on a one-way street, this is a good idea; I've seen cars going the wrong way all too often).

You also can't go back to somewhere you've been before and expect it to be the same. For visitors to the Louvre before I. M. Pei designed the glass pyramid at the entrance, the former palace turned art museum looks entirely different; I'm of the school that believes it looked better without the pyramid, but there is the other school that thinks it's brilliant. I've read about the controversy, but my observations and opinions are based on seeing it for myself. I'm thrilled that I have firsthand knowledge.

Naturally, no one can see everything. But the more you see, the better you know where you fall on various issues, and the better educated and sophisticated you become in sifting through points of view disseminated by the media.

While familiarity with a destination is useful, don't assume that everything is going to be the same because that likely won't be the case. In one of my early trips to Paris, I visited the Jeu de Paume when it held the best Impressionist art. On a later trip, the collection had been moved to the Musée d'Orsay, a former train station. Though I adore trains and train stations, and I like buildings when they are adapted to new uses, the Jeu de Paume was so intimate and charming that I was disappointed by the new home for the Impressionist art.

I've made two trips to Versailles. While the palace is still unbelievable, on my second visit I got a chance to wander around much more of the estate and was fascinated by the other homes on the property, and the world unto itself that exists away from the main structure.

On that second visit, I just got to see more. To my knowledge, nothing had changed except the extent to which I explored. Since I'd previously seen the inside of the palace, I had time to absorb more of the visual input on the surrounding estate.

Taking Reasonable Risks

Reasonable is a subjective term. On my first trip to Europe, which I did solo, I met another American woman staying at the same hotel where a travel agent had booked my stay. We became travel buddies for a few days. She was off to other countries after that and asked if I wanted to travel with her. I was headed back to the States and declined, which I now regret.

We kept in touch for a few years, corresponding about our lives. She took up skydiving, met her husband who was also a skydiver, and changed her life. I did my own things, which to many might seem risky. But I can't imagine myself ever jumping out of a plane . . . voluntarily, at least.

I read a book about risk some time ago. In it, the author explained that what challenges and scares some of us, seems like nothing to someone else. I enjoy public speaking; I get excited "being on stage." For me, I leave the skydiving, motorcycles, and bungee jumping to others—these things are much riskier to me than speaking in front of a large group.

For our purposes here, taking reasonable risks means seeking adventure without ignoring the State Department's warnings for dangerous areas, without traveling to the Caribbean or South Florida in the midst of a hurricane, without getting on a flight during a tornado warning.

This happened to me once in Orlando. A series of tornadoes had hit the area, but the airline did not cancel its flights. I never even went to the airport that day, determined to stay safe even if I had to pay for an extra hotel night and a new flight. As it turned out, others who went to the airport sat in the terminal for hours, at which point the airline actually did cancel all flights out that day. Meanwhile, I had a relaxing afternoon around the hotel pool, having decided that my peace of mind was worth any extra expense.

When I met Christiane Amanpour, CNN's chief international correspondent, I asked her if she is ever scared when she is visiting a war-torn country. She told me that she doesn't think about it. She was impressive, treating me with the same respect she gives to world leaders, for which I was grateful. But I could never personally go to the places she goes and take the risks she takes. That's another reason it's fascinating to listen to her—she's out there researching what's going on for the rest of us.

In my conversations with people about this book, many told me that they like reading about adventures they would never personally take. But sometimes, when they do read about a seemingly challenging exploit, they think, "I could do that." I almost feel that way about scaling Mt. Kilimanjaro, a journey I learned about through a man I know. After he explained to me the steps involved in planning and training, I thought, "I could do that." If something you hear or read stimulates an interest, follow that dream. You never know what excitement you'll find.

> *If something you hear or read stimulates an interest, follow that dream. You never know what excitement you'll find.*

Meeting or Seeing Celebrities

It's often fun to see someone famous when you're traveling. I tend to remember where I was at various "sightings."

For instance, I was outside the Breakers resort in Palm Beach, Florida, when Celine Dion arrived in a white limo. And I was in the lobby of the Four Seasons hotel in Washington, DC, when I noticed a crowd. Robin Williams, dressed all in black and wearing glasses, was in the midst of the crowd.

I was on a plane from Washington, DC, to Boston, sitting in coach and amusing myself while a woman across the aisle put on makeup. I was thinking about my upcoming stay in Boston and only half paying attention. "There are several members of Congress onboard this flight," the woman confided in me.

"Really? Who?" I asked.

"Well, me for one," she said.

"Who are you?" I asked.

The senator introduced herself to me.

"Oh my God, I'm so sorry not to have recognized you," I said, embarrassed.

"That's okay, there are a hundred of us."

"But there aren't that many women," I said. "I should have recognized you." She went on to tell me about the other politicians who were onboard. In Boston, they were filming the events surrounding the final episode of *Cheers*; several politicians from Capitol Hill were flying into Logan Airport to appear on television.

I became more politically aware after that encounter, challenging myself to learn to recognize as many U.S. senators as possible. Next time I'm sitting next to a senator on a plane, I'll be ready to ask policy questions. Hopefully the senator might just want to answer.

I've thought about that encounter many times. I'm convinced that the senator realized I didn't recognize her, so she let me know who she was. I'm sure she doesn't remember the incident. But I'll never forget it.

On one of my other trips to Boston, I actually visited the original Bull and Finch Pub that served as the inspiration for the television show *Cheers*. I'll never forget that visit either. After all, situation comedies have become an integral part of our culture, of watercooler conversation.

I bought a *Cheers* shot glass on that visit. It's on the top shelf of my kitchen cabinet. I never use it. But I know it's there. That's what souvenirs are often about.

Timing Is Everything

In travel, as in life, timing is everything. Public transport runs on a schedule. There may be delays due to mechanical or weather-related causes, but a plane or train will not wait for you.

I have been seen running through an airport with heavy luggage in tow, having planned poorly, overpacked, and arrived late. With security getting ever more stringent, and having been miserable when I planned so badly, I've gotten better about leaving extra time. Going to an airport or train station, you may have trouble getting a taxi or finding parking for your car, or you may run into traffic on the way. Leaving extra time is a great concept. Packing carefully is another one.

Talking to Strangers

As children, we're taught to look both ways when crossing the street, hold onto an adult's hand, and not to talk to strangers.

We're adults now and traveling solo gives us a great opportunity to pursue our personal interests, sleep, rest, relax, have a change of scenery, *and* talk to strangers.

Of course, there was the adult man who sat next to me on a flight to Florida; he was clinging to a teddy bear the entire time. I was particularly glad when that flight landed.

Learning About New Things

On a train trip into Manhattan, I had an interesting conversation with a man who told me all about "geocaching." This "sport" is done worldwide with handheld Global Positioning System (GPS) devices as a kind of treasure hunt where the hunt is more of a factor than the treasure. Apparently, it's a worldwide phenomenon among some travelers. The man told me that he does it often when he's traveling by himself. When he's near home, he participates with his wife and sons.

Geocaching entails locating a "cache" where baubles or notes are left, keeping track of the find, and then proceeding to the next "cache." Clues are found on the Internet.

A business associate told me she just came back from a vacation in which she went "snuba-ing." I thought she was mispronouncing scuba diving, or that I misheard her. I asked her to repeat it. Then I asked her to spell it. She explained that it's a cross between scuba diving and snorkeling. Participants swim underwater using diving masks and breathing equipment like those used in scuba diving, but the air tanks remain on rafts at the water's surface. Thus, swimmers stay relatively close to the surface, no more than twenty feet down, which is, of course, further down than if they were snorkeling.

I never knew about either of these activities before, but now that I'm more aware, their existence adds to the many options for future travel.

Picking Your Battles

Don't take the hassles personally. In this age of heightened security, it is important to realize that you are not being singled out if security or customs officials ask extra questions or decide to search your person or belongings.

On my first trip to Detroit on business, my client had booked me on two one-way tickets, which is often a trigger for extra scrutiny. As a result, I got searched on the way there and was warned that it would happen to me again when I was leaving Detroit. So I was somewhat prepared. What did surprise me in Detroit, however, was when a heavyset female Transportation Security Administration (TSA) agent grabbed my breasts and squeezed. "What are you doing?" I objected rather loudly.

"The underwire on your bra went off," she answered.

"I'm not wearing a bra," I protested, my indignation overcoming any concern I might otherwise have had for an "official" in a security role. I complained to one of the male agents, and he went and got a female manager. When I told the manager what happened, she laughed. I couldn't believe it. She suggested I come into a private room to file a report. I asked why I couldn't file a report out in the open and she laughed again.

At that point I said, "Never mind" and decided to cut my losses. I didn't want to go into a back room somewhere. And I didn't want to miss my flight.

Right after that, there were media reports about similar instances. At a party, I told the story to some women who are apparently tougher than I am. They told me they would have kicked her or told her off in various ways. The men to whom I told the story insisted that if an agent grabbed them in a comparable fashion, that agent would be sorry.

If I had reacted in one of the ways everyone suggested, I might have gotten myself arrested. Besides, I'm glad that the TSA is working to protect us. However, I began to wonder if perhaps I gave off a vibe that I would react passively, making me a target to that deviant agent. I was definitely not on guard. I had no contraband, I was being searched routinely, and I wasn't paying much attention. That was my mistake.

That day in the Detroit airport, I was with business colleagues. When I'm on my own, I'm often more alert and usually manage to avoid some of this nonsense.

If you are stopped for a special search, be on guard. That's the important thing. When you're distracted, which is easy to do while traveling, stuff happens.

Chapter 8

FROM HOTEL GUEST TO HOUSEGUEST

A place to sleep may seem unimportant when you're excited about catching a Broadway show or the sunrise over a mountain or the ocean, but travel and time-zone changes are disorienting. Where you choose to stay, plus the amenities or hardships included, does make a difference. A comfortable mattress versus a mat on the floor, the need to be gracious to a host who is a friend or to fellow guests at a bed and breakfast (B&B), certainly differs compared to the comfortable anonymity of a huge resort.

Deciding whether to use your entire budget, or to find a deal that leaves extra money to spend, alters the landscape of a trip. Your choice may also alter a trip as it relates to relaxation and enthusiasm. Beware of making trade-offs too readily. Sometimes it's worth a little discomfort to save money; other times it's worth investing a bit more to indulge. You're on your own, so ultimately, it is all up to you whether you share a bathroom or a meal, or choose to enjoy your own company and counsel. All this, plus more, should filter into your decision making.

Being Pampered and Indulged

Indulgence is individual. Someone told me that her idea of "roughing it" is staying in a hotel without twenty-four-hour room service.

I once stayed at the St. Regis Hotel, in New York City, where I had twenty-four-hour butler service. I was so intimidated, I was afraid to use it. I didn't want someone else unpacking my clothes. And I didn't know how to behave.

But curiosity got the best of me. I could conquer this, I thought. I called and asked for a cup of tea. Later I asked for a band-aid and for help putting on a bracelet with a tricky catch. The butler quickly put me at ease, and I started fantasizing about a life in which all I had to do was ask for my bath to be drawn.

Obviously, I don't need a butler for a cup of tea or a band-aid. Maybe it takes time getting used to being pampered. Maybe I'm just not cut out to have a butler, though a friend recently pointed out that "butlers" in upscale hotels are really only extensions of room service. He's right, but the term "butler" carries extra cachet.

Sometimes pampering is just not having to make the bed in the morning, having a newspaper left at the front door, receiving a wake-up call by a cheerful person who tells you the weather, finding fancy soaps in the bathroom or a pair of slippers left by the bed as part of turn-down service. Pampering can be not having to do household chores or taking time off from work.

Other times pampering entails eating out in luxurious surroundings, getting a massage, and working out with a private trainer. It can be eating a hot dog at a ball game where you don't have to grill the hot dog yourself, or having someone in a diner make you a grilled cheese sandwich just the way you like it.

Walking down a street in New York City, when I don't have to be anywhere in particular, is a treat for me, because I can wander in and out of stores and people watch at my leisure. Walking on a beach off-season when it's cold and relatively deserted is also a treat for me. I like champagne and caviar, but I also love a smoothie at the beach and a slice of pizza at a basketball game.

Luxury in a Countryside Castle

It wasn't on my radar screen at all. I would have chosen other places to visit first. But a good friend spent a weekend in Dublin and told me he liked it. Then I was invited to join other journalists on a weeklong visit to Ireland. I figured, why not. My friend told me I would enjoy it, for everyone in Ireland seems to have many stories to tell.

Often we look forward to travel so much that we're disappointed. Or we travel without expectation and have a marvelous experience. Ireland was, for me, that wonderfully unexpected time.

Although I was with a small group of strangers, my favorite times on that trip were when I went off alone. I took a fly-fishing lesson with a ghillie (guide) in a small boat out in the middle of Lough Corrib, and the beauty and quiet of the lake were memorable. I also took a private golf lesson on a nine-hole course at Ashford Castle overlooking the lough (lake).

I didn't really learn to cast, and I certainly didn't improve my golf game, but I had a delightful time nonetheless. During the golf lesson, it was raining softly and quietly but I could have cared less. I was alive and excited, and I recommend golf lessons in the rain if you are lucky enough to be in Ireland, staying at a castle in the countryside.

Making Good Use of the Concierge

A good concierge can provide invaluable assistance. Luxury hotels often have the best professionals staffing their concierge desk, but other, more mid-level properties can provide good service too. Even in budget hotels and motels, or small bed and breakfasts, getting friendly with the front-desk staff or manager can give you a local source for useful information.

What can you ask? Well, make sure it's legal; otherwise, the sky's the limit. Concierges have been known to arrange helicopters, emergency clothes for guests in need of a business suit or a pair of shoes, party plans, travel plans, tickets to sold-out events, restaurant reservations, and much more.

Even in budget hotels and motels, or small bed and breakfasts, getting friendly with the front-desk staff or manager can give you a local source for useful information.

If a concierge is wearing a pin with two crossed keys, that means he or she is a member of *Les Clefs d'Or,* or the Golden Keys. More than likely, if that is the case, you're in good hands. But not all wonderful concierges have this designation, so don't be surprised if you get what you need from a concierge who does not sport the pin.

Sometimes the concierges are so busy that they can't spend time with you. Usually, however, you'll get at least competent assistance and often much more.

Unlike my intimidation with a butler, I often and readily ask for information and opinions from a concierge. I don't always follow the advice dispensed, but I use it as input along with information from other sources. After all, a concierge is only providing an opinion, albeit an educated one. With restaurants, for instance, I recently asked a concierge to print out menus from the Internet for restaurants he was recommending to me. After looking at the menus, it was clear that his recommendations were more formal and high priced than what I wanted for dinner on my own.

Instead, I ended up at Bess, a restaurant in downtown Austin owned by Sandra Bullock. It was a delightful, casual restaurant with reasonable prices. Everyone was friendly, and I satisfied my curiosity about her restaurant. I had a good time, which is all I wanted.

African Safaris

Living in a tent and going on safari sounded like roughing it to me until I spoke with a friend who has taken several safaris (the photographic, not the hunting kind) and plans to go on several more. After talking with him about it, I've put it on my "to do" list.

He says it is great because you get to see animals that you learn about when you are a child—animals such as elephants, tigers, leopards, cheetahs, and lions, as well as others like wildebeests. It is a popular kind of trek, and it is easy to go it alone as no one does a safari without guides. Since you join up with a group anyway, it doesn't matter whether you are part of a couple or a solo traveler.

You fly to Africa and get off the plane, where you hook up with a prearranged tour group. From there, you are driven in jeeps from park to park. No one walks around because of the wild animals, and you ride in different kinds of jeeps because of safety issues. The kind of jeep depends upon the kind of animals in the particular park you are visiting. A man in the jeep rides shotgun with a rifle, just in case.

For accommodations, you might be in a tent or you might be in a small cottage overlooking a lake. You may even be able to watch animals in the morning from a private veranda.

If you are in a tent, there may be a wooden floor and an indoor commode. Within the lodge area, you are protected from animal attacks by electrified barbed wire. There will be a lock on your door, and you dine on prepared meals. It's not the height of luxury, but it's not exactly roughing it either.

Affordable Luxury at a Discount

Lots of us love to travel, but we don't have unlimited funds. Still, luxurious travel is loads of fun and there is a way to enjoy it without breaking the bank. In fact, if you are clever and plan way in advance or at the last minute (it's the extremes that often offer great deals), you can enjoy luxury for not much more than regular price.

One way to do this is to travel off-season. This doesn't mean you have to be in the Caribbean with a hurricane bearing down. But it does mean going when it's not an optimum time because it's probably still warm where you live, and even warmer on whatever island you choose.

Beaches that are further north, such as those stretching from Virginia to Maine, can be great places to go in the fall—usually at the end of October when prices are slashed but it's not yet wintertime. Try going yourself. Feel the mood and enjoy the luxuries off-season.

In cities, such as New York and Washington, DC, where business travel raises the cost of hotel rooms, there are often deals to be had on weekends. In a place, such as Las Vegas, where leisure travel is more the norm, deals can often be had at hotels on weekdays, although the convention business can throw off that schedule.

When dining, if you want to go to a fancy restaurant, it's almost always cheaper if you dine there at lunchtime instead of for dinner. If you splurge for one meal, grab a sandwich for the next or get a drink during happy hour when they are serving free appetizers. Many luxury hotels offer free food on the concierge level, so even though the rooms may cost more, you might be able to save on your food bill.

Booking airfare far in advance of a travel date, or upgrading with frequent flyer points, might allow you to fly business class, which is infinitely more comfortable than coach, as it offers extra leg room, better food, and often such amenities as individual DVD players for each flyer. Booking luxury hotel rooms at the last minute might allow you to get a deluxe room or suite for a much reduced cost. Just make sure to have a backup plan so you end up with at least someplace to sleep.

To go to the theater in London's West End or on New York's Broadway, search out half price ticket booths on the day of the show. For specials in a place like Las Vegas, ask at check-in if the hotel has any dining or show specials, or if they can provide you with any complimentary tickets; frequently these are available just for the asking.

If your idea of pleasure is to have a full body massage at a spa, book one in the city where you live. Take the day off and pretend you're on vacation. The massage may be $100 or more, but you'll save the cost of airfare and a hotel, so the massage will be well worth the splurge.

There are many ways to indulge yourself without a high price tag. However, if you are truly looking to treat yourself and you can afford it, do so. When you are alone, it might make the difference between a good trip and a terrific one. After all, sometimes it's not where you go but how you're treated along the way that makes a trip special.

Sometimes it's the things that don't cost an extra cent that make all the difference—a warm tropical breeze, a child's smile, and impromptu street theater.

Then again, sometimes it's the things that don't cost an extra cent that make all the difference—a warm tropical breeze, a child's smile, and impromptu street theater all come to mind. Look out for your own personal moments. And enjoy.

Enjoying Visits to Friends and Relatives . . . Really

The best way to become a good houseguest is to have people stay in your home. You can see what they do to annoy you and make an effort to avoid those things when you're visiting someone else.

For instance, one of my houseguests kept leaving a wet towel on the bed, on top of an expensive comforter. I asked her to stop, but she argued that the wet towel wouldn't hurt the comforter. Maybe not, but it was my house, my comforter, my towel, and the water from my shower. All she needed to say was, "Okay."

Then there are the houseguests who want to use my computer. I know they just want to check their e-mail and I don't mind exactly. But I'm reminded of the *Friends* episode where Joey opens a suspect e-mail and loses Ross' speech. After all, I'm a writer, and my laptop affects my livelihood.

I'm also really careful to avoid putting a cup of coffee or a can of soda near my computer where I might accidentally knock it over. I work at the computer a lot, and I've learned the hard way to leave my drink on the floor next to my desk. Then when I knock it over, which I inevitably do on occasion, the carpet suffers but not my computer or the papers on my desk. This rule has not always gone over well with my houseguests, but on this one I am insistent and I do not waver. The guests who really mind have finally gotten the idea that they ought to bring their own laptop with them. If they use mine, they must play by my rules.

When You Have Houseguests

- ✔ Change the sheets, and make sure you let your guest know you've changed them.
- ✔ Make sure you have food in the fridge and something to drink—whether it's just Coke or bottled water doesn't matter, but do have something other than tap water.
- ✔ Clean and spruce up the bathroom. This is a good time to put out those little soaps and other amenities that you collected last time you were at a hotel or bought at a holiday fair. Make sure to put out fresh towels too; this includes hand towels that hang in your guest (or your own, if your place is small) bathroom. A vase with fresh flowers is another nice touch.
- ✔ Make your guest feel welcome. However, you don't need to let a guest borrow your car, computer, clothes, or jewelry—that goes above and beyond.
- ✔ If your guest wants to treat you to dinner or for tickets to a show, accept graciously.
- ✔ You don't need to stop your life. You can go to work, play with your kids, and walk the dog. Try to include your houseguest whenever possible, but as long as you communicate the things you need to do in advance, your houseguest should be able to entertain himself.
- ✔ If you have certain house rules, tell your friend up front. Try not to have too many rules. After all, your guest is probably only staying a few days.

On Being a Houseguest

I've had good and bad experiences being a houseguest. The bad ones tend to make the best stories, so I'll start with one of those:

I got a last-minute client project while on my way cross-country to visit a friend. I brought my laptop and stayed up late working in my friend's home office. She had a really large home, and her office was in a separate wing from her bedroom. Around 1 a.m., she came into her office, angry. It seems her dog, who slept in her room, was sick and made noises that woke her up. Realizing that I was awake, she insisted that I had to go to bed immediately, otherwise she would not be able to go back to sleep.

Instead of arguing, I took my laptop into the guest bedroom, quietly closed the door, and continued working on the bed. What she didn't know didn't hurt her. I finished my work around 3 a.m. and was able to e-mail it to my client the next morning.

This same host got annoyed with me for closing the guest bathroom door and leaving the guest bedroom door open. Apparently she likes it in reverse—an open bathroom door and a closed bedroom one. Okay. Next time, present me with a list of rules, I thought, though of course there will not be a next time at her house.

When my friends get unreasonable, I sometimes joke, "Tell me where that appears in the rulebook." I'm not suggesting that's particularly politic or that you should imitate it, but it does make me feel better.

I spent a lovely time visiting the home of a fellow travel writer in upstate New York. She had a large, lovely house, was a good cook, loved to sit and talk, and was receptive to showing me around the area. Although she had pets and I like pets, she did not foist hers on me, which I appreciated. Like people, pets sometimes require familiarity before warmth ensues. Perhaps that was my best experience as a houseguest. I think that's because she was used to traveling, to adjusting herself to other situations, and was thus flexible in her acceptance of my habits, and I of hers.

I always offer to take my hosts out to dinner as my treat. When visiting relatives in Florida, I did this. We went out to eat, but they generously insisted on paying the check. I tried to object, but they were obviously more comfortable treating me, so I let it go. You can always follow up with a small gift, but it's easier and more immediate when the person or persons I'm visiting let me treat for dinner.

To be a good houseguest, try to stay below the radar.

To be a good houseguest, try to stay below the radar. Don't drive your hosts crazy, and don't let them drive you crazy. Appreciate the fact that staying in someone's home is nicer, in many ways, than staying in a hotel where you are paying for everything. To whatever extent, your hosts are going out of their way for you, are extending their home to you, and are saying they value their relationship with you.

Bringing a Gift

There are lots of choices for appropriate and thoughtful house gifts, and they need not be expensive. I generally prefer bringing something with me, thus saving me the trouble of sending something later, or getting busy and letting it slip by. But bringing something requires preparation.

The better you know the people you're visiting, the easier it is to capture just the right creativity. But it need not be complicated. Food, wine, a book, gourmet coffee, or a DVD—all are perfectly acceptable. After all, the goal is not to spend as much as you would have on a hotel room. In this situation, it *is* the thought that counts.

Try to target the gift to each recipient's likes or dislikes. If he loves to barbecue, buy him an appropriate cookbook. If she loves Chardonnay, don't bring her a Bordeaux.

If those you're visiting have kids or pets, you might gift the child or pet instead of the parents. Yo-yos or a paint set for young children will make their parents smile. Dog biscuits and a pull toy for the golden retriever will let them know you appreciate that Rover is a beloved member of their family. When you close your door at night so Rover can't jump in bed with you, having brought him a gift will ameliorate your preference for sleeping alone.

Be Careful About Re-gifting

On the subject of re-gifts, be careful. A friend brought a gift for me when she came to town and stayed with me. Without revealing too much, it was obvious that I was being re-gifted. As they discuss on *Seinfeld,* re-gifting has its own set of rules. However, she did make the gesture, and I suspect she was unaware that the re-gifting was so obvious.

It's okay to do re-gifting, but don't make it obvious. Make sure:

- ✔ You remove any previous gift cards;
- ✔ The recipients aren't the ones who gave you the gift in the first place;
- ✔ You sincerely believe your hosts will like the gift better than you did (otherwise give it to a charity);
- ✔ The gift is not a generic brand of candy or month-old vintage of wine that is nowhere near ready to be consumed. Godiva might not be the best candy in the world, but its name has

cachet. A small box of Godiva, or a light blue Tiffany box with a token gift, will generally appeal to recipients. Brands do count in this situation.

Note: If you often travel on the spur of the moment and tend to stay with friends and family, you may want to buy a few gifts in advance so you always have something handy. This will help avoid last-minute shopping.

If You Want to Be Invited Back
- ✔ Don't tell the person you're visiting that your home is nicer, larger, more expensive, or whatever than theirs. Don't complain about the mattress or the size of the TV. Find something to compliment—the artwork, the view, the kitchen appliances, anything. Don't overdo it, but be nice.
- ✔ Clean up after yourself.
- ✔ Don't plan to borrow clothes.
- ✔ Bring your own computer and cell phone if you think you'll need them.
- ✔ Rent your own car if you'll need one.
- ✔ Always try to hang wet towels on a towel rack or over the shower.
- ✔ Don't monopolize the bathroom if you're sharing it.
- ✔ Smile and have a good time. Include your hosts in at least one activity—dinner, breakfast, sightseeing, whatever. You can't expect them to spend every minute with you, but you don't want to ignore them either. This is not a hotel or a B&B.
- ✔ Show up when you are expected to arrive and make sure you leave when you said you would. If you have a good reason for being late, at least call. If you need to stay longer than anticipated, consider moving to a hotel so as not to overstay your welcome.
- ✔ Don't expect your hosts to cook and clean for you.

Breakfast, You Want Breakfast?
I visited a friend who told me she likes English muffins for breakfast and wanted to know what I like. I said an English muffin would be fine, to which she replied, "I only have one left."

I suggested we stop at the grocery store on the way home from the restaurant (where I had treated for dinner) so that I could buy something for breakfast. We did that, but she complained that had she known, she would have brought her weekly shopping list along. I bought extra food and left it in her refrigerator when I flew out two days later.

We had been friends for several years, but by staying with her, I saw a side that I didn't know was there. She effectively gave me a crash course on how not to behave when I have houseguests of my own. She also taught me to appreciate the friends and relatives who graciously invite me into their homes and treat me well, clearly enjoying my company and welcoming my presence.

Someone once asked me, "Where do you get these people?" I have some great friends, but then there are these other . . . characters, I'll call them. They are the ones who give me plenty of stories to tell.

Chapter 9

NEGOTIATING AND PLAYING IT SMART

Deciding to travel alone means that unless you're tagging leisure travel onto a business trip, which is one great way of traveling, you'll be picking up the check. Whatever your finances, there's no reason to pay more than necessary. Here are some useful tips on getting the best deals possible.

Knowledge Is Powerful

It *is* a fact that hotels lose revenue for any and all unsold rooms. Therefore, high occupancy is always a goal in the hotel industry. You can sometimes negotiate a better rate if you call a hotel directly rather than using the Internet or a chain's 800 number.

Hotel executives have told me that sometimes you can walk into a hotel without a reservation on the evening you want to check in and get a deal on the spot. Beware, however, that some hotels may be totally booked on any given night, though there may be last-minute cancellations. Having a backup plan is a good idea in case this doesn't work so that you're not out on the street or forced to settle for undesirable accommodations.

One of my relatives called ahead to the west coast of Florida for a reservation. The woman with whom she spoke told her that the hotel was not busy and that my relative could get a better rate by just walking in. That's what she did, and she was able to get her hotel accommodations at bargain prices.

Holiday seasons are often quiet in hotels, with many families staying at home or visiting relatives. Check in advance to see if there will be many vacancies; if there will be, you might want to just walk in.

Perseverance Helps

On the French Riviera, I had to drive from town to town before I could find an available room one Saturday night. That turned out okay, though it was late by the time I got settled in, and there were few options left for dinner at that hour. I didn't have a backup plan, and I had not done advance research; if I had, I would have learned that weekends in the popular coastal towns are often busy. Next time, I will do things differently.

I wouldn't want to be stuck in New York City at 10 p.m. without a place to stay, especially now that many of that city's hotel rooms are being converted into apartments for purchase by foreign buyers benefiting from the weakened dollar. But if you have a backup plan, walking into a hotel the night you want to stay may allow you to get accommodations at less-than-usual cost. Just know that this may be difficult in busy places like New York, Chicago, or L.A.

Asking about last-minute availabilities can work well if you're already booked into a hotel with a generous cancellation policy. If you find a more desirable hotel nearby before you check in with your existing reservation, it might be worth asking what kind of deal you can get.

I never like to pay for more than a few nights in advance. I once moved from a hotel in Dutch St. Maarten to a more charming hotel in French St. Martin on the other side of the island. Upon arrival, I quickly found that I preferred the French side to the Dutch—perhaps because I speak some French, but also because the Dutch town was where the cruise ships docked, and it was highly commercial, whereas the French town was less crowded and more relaxed.

At the Dutch hotel, I only had a tiny room with a closet-sized bathroom. The French hotel was far nicer, with a charming interior courtyard, large tiled guest rooms, and beautiful flowers everywhere. And yet, the French hotel had the added advantage of being less expensive.

Flexibility is always a good bargaining tool. Since I was on holiday by myself, I just had to make sure the new hotel had an available room. I even got to see the room before I made my decision, before

---

TIP

Places do have personality; the trick (as with people) is in getting to know them. Don't be fooled by a place's best foot being put forward. Get beyond superficial beauty or excitement, to the real heart and soul of the people and the characteristics unique to a place.

I picked up and moved. Repacking took only a few minutes, and it was an easy taxi ride, so the change was virtually stress-free. With ten days on the island, I ended up staying on the French side six nights since I had only prepaid for three nights on the Dutch side. By staying on both sides of the island, I learned more about what I like and dislike. I also got a chance to really get to know the place and to see firsthand how its dual nationality plays a huge role in its personality.

Things to Negotiate

Cost. This is the first thing most people try to change—the cost of a hotel room, taxi ride, boat ride, or souvenir in an open-air market. Actually, everything's negotiable. Well, almost. However, if you really want or need something, recognize that the other person in the negotiation has the power. Bluffing sometimes helps. But don't get so caught up in the gamesmanship that you walk away from something you really want. There's no shame in paying full price if you've tried to negotiate without any luck.

I had a client who asked me to write two brochures for his company. He warned me that he always haggles and would never pay full price. Knowing this in advance, I marked up my price 20 percent. He negotiated me down 10 percent, so I was ahead of the game by 10 percent.

I've thought about this often and have come to the conclusion that he handed me that piece of information because he knew himself well and feared discouraging me from doing work he wanted me to do. He purposely told me to mark up my price so he could feel like a winner by knocking it down. What he didn't anticipate was that I would go up as much as I did. Therein is the answer to the game— the best way to win a negotiation is to do the unexpected.

Don't confuse the game of bargaining with a desire to obtain things you really want. As long as you realize that the two differ, you'll be happier—both when traveling and in other aspects of life. Negotiation tactics you've learned at home or in business are certainly applicable in travel situations. The main lesson is that it doesn't hurt to ask for something you want; it's often easy for a hotel manager or tour guide to grant your wish.

Amenities. If you can't affect the price, no matter how hard you try negotiating, see if you can get breakfast included in the price, a bottle of wine sent to the room, or free use of the hotel health club if there's usually an extra charge. Free parking is another easily negotiated perk, as is a glass of wine or dessert in a restaurant.

In Las Vegas, for instance, it's really easy for a manager to "comp" (provide "comp"-limentary or free) a meal if your room is not ready when it's supposed to be, or to provide free tickets to a show. Sometimes all you have to do is ask, even if your room is ready and there are no problems. After all, comps are part of the infrastructure in Las Vegas, the *modus operandi* used by management to court high rollers.

Even if you're not a gambler, or if you're like me, and you limit yourself to $50 at the blackjack table and another $20 in the slots, comps are part of the culture.

I once negotiated a free night and a free meal when I arrived in Las Vegas after midnight with a guaranteed reservation. They checked me into a room that had not been cleaned. There was even an unflushed toilet. Since they were sold-out, I had to wait an hour for housekeeping to work its magic rather than being able to switch into another room. I negotiated with the manager and got the night free as well as a comped meal. I would have preferred to go right to sleep on clean sheets at full price, but as long as I was inconvenienced due to the hotel's slip-up, I felt better knowing that I was not paying for my lost bedtime.

Friends of mine went to a casino hotel in Atlantic City recently. I suggested they ask for freebies at check-in. "Don't you have to gamble a certain amount?" my friend hesitated.

"Maybe," I said. "But it doesn't hurt to ask." Our conversation was longer than this, as I really had to coax her to help me with my research. But she did, and the manager said he couldn't give her much—just six free drink tickets for her and her husband. It took all of twenty seconds for them to get thirty dollars worth of drinks.

"I just said, what kind of goodies have you got for us this time?" she reported to me.

I asked, will she do it again?

"Absolutely."

Upgrades. These are especially useful if you are a frequent traveler with an airline or hotel chain. Even if you don't have enough clout (that is points) to qualify for the best treatment, it's worth asking for perks anyway. A company representative might be able to do something for you, or find you a special deal. It might make sense to purchase a small number of points if you're close to the total you'll need. Short flights are sometimes available at a reduced number of points. If you have a long layover at an airport, use of the airline's club lounge can make your time there more pleasant. Upgrades or lounge usage require fewer points than a free flight.

If you're staying at a hotel for several nights and don't mind moving mid-visit, keep asking if a suite has become available. Often you can get a room upgrade with a little friendly persistence.

Asking More Than Once

Late checkout. If the desk clerk says "no" to stretching your room hours, try calling back later when the night shift is on duty, or vice versa. If your flight doesn't leave until evening, it's great to have a base of operations later than noon on your day of departure. Sometimes the first desk clerk will offer an extra hour. If you call back on the next shift and speak with someone else, that hour can frequently be extended even further.

Early check-in. Often you can negotiate an early check-in just by asking; this works best if you are traveling off-season and only want an extra hour or two. On the other hand, it might be smart to add an extra day at the beginning of your hotel reservation if you absolutely need to get into the hotel in the morning upon arrival. Someone I know always pays for an extra "first" day in Europe. Taking the plane overnight, she wants to get to her hotel at 8 a.m., sleep until noon, and then she is ready for her visit without having jetlag. If you can afford to do this, it is a luxury you might not want to miss. You'll need to let the hotel know your plans in advance, however, and guarantee the room. Otherwise hotel employees might assume you're not coming and give your room to another guest.

Free transportation in the hotel limo. You normally need to be at an upscale property to find this perk, which is sometimes available at downtown hotels. I was able to make use of a hotel town car in Houston, for instance, when I was in that city for a conference. Since I was not staying at the designated conference hotel, I made lots of trips via the town car from the hotel where I was staying. I made sure to tip the driver well each time; as a result, he was always glad to see me any time I needed a ride during the three or four days of my stay.

Finding a Deal

One of the reasons some people give for never traveling alone is the expense. After all, two people can stay in a hotel room for the same relative cost as one, two people can stay in a cabin on a cruise, two people can use the same rental car, or even share a dinner entrée. Sometimes though, buying one ticket allows you to obtain a lower cost. If you're booking only one airline or theater ticket, you might qualify for a lower cost tier, whereas two or more seats together may be available only in a higher tier.

Some people travel with less than ideal companions just to have someone with whom to split costs. This even happens at business conferences, with virtual strangers sometimes sharing accommodations.

When a traveling companion makes a trip more special, that's great. When a traveling companion is just there to save you money, that is not so great. While waiting for a flight at JFK Airport in New York, I struck up a conversation with an elderly woman. She told me that she recently lost her husband. Even before he died, she confided in me that she had not traveled with him.

She proceeded to tell me about a memorable trip she took to France. Her brother and sister-in-law were with her, but as usual, her husband hadn't wanted to go. She planned to go with a friend too, but her friend was in a car accident just before the scheduled trip, so this woman went what she called "alone." With her brother and sister-in-law there, that wasn't exactly true, but she often separated from them when in Paris and Versailles, as well as when they toured Normandy.

"When I got home, my husband didn't even want to hear about the trip. I'm so glad he didn't go with me. There's nothing worse than being with someone who doesn't want to be there."

Timing Is Often Everything

Traveling alone provides increased flexibility. After all, you only have to satisfy one set of needs, not two. This can include timing—how far in advance you plan or how last minute you are willing to decide before you go. Both extremes can offer financial deals—planning way in advance or going at the last minute. Most travelers opt for something in the middle, so if you are willing to buck the norm, you can probably travel less expensively.

The same is true of "off-season" travel. If you go to many northern U.S. beaches before Memorial Day or after Labor Day, you can save money. Florida beaches and other points south will be in reverse. Off-season travel also provides the least hassle—without crowds, lines, or traffic.

It is good to research the place you're planning to visit. I wouldn't want to go to Europe in August, for instance, when many Europeans are on holiday—it's just too busy. But late September is one of my favorite times there; the weather is still nice and the crowds are much diminished.

Foreign Languages . . . and Other Versions of English

Phrase books, a few choice words, as well as written hotel addresses and phone numbers are indispensable. While you cannot reasonably become proficient in Mandarin before visiting Beijing, it doesn't hurt to know words like "please," "help," or "thank you" in whatever language is spoken where you'll be going.

There are many variations within any language. Someone from Havana, Cuba, will speak Spanish differently than someone from Madrid, Spain, or Buenos Aires, Argentina. So too, just because the language is English, don't assume you will understand everything.

In England, for instance, I learned that "having a bit of a kip," means you've taken a nap. Other British terms include: queue (line), bloke (man), loo (restroom), biscuit (cookie), lift (elevator), boot (car trunk), chips (fries), and torch (flashlight).

I've been to Texas many times. On one trip I met someone from a small town there; she had an accent, and I couldn't understand a word she said. Everyone else was laughing at a joke she told; I was laughing at my inability to understand English as spoken in parts of the United States.

A Little Research Goes a Long Way

For the most part, I believe in winging it. However, it is a good idea to learn that a quid is the same as a British pound, which is made up of 100 pence just like we have 100 pennies to a dollar.

When you hear that, "David Beckham is the world's best football player," that translates to soccer player in the United States. Our football is American football to the rest of the world, and soccer is football.

All these linguistic differences exist even in an English-speaking nation where we have a lot in common. Imagine the differences in another language with a more divergent culture from ours.

Playing It Smart

While you want to get bargains and not spend more money than necessary, going it alone needs to be approached differently from traveling with someone else. When I'm in the U.S., I'll happily rent a car and drive myself wherever I want to go. But when I'm in another country, that is not my idea of fun, especially in countries where they drive on the left-hand side.

To avoid driving in a foreign country by myself, I have options. I can hire a driver/guide. I can also take public transport—taxis, buses, and trains.

Hiring a Guide

I used to think it was a cop-out to hire a guide. But that was when my journeys took me to places like London and Paris.

Now that I've branched out, I realize there are places where it is smart to hire someone to show you around, especially if your time is limited. After all, what is the point in declaring your independence by trying to get around without a guide, only to miss the very sites you want to see because you couldn't negotiate a foreign language or a foreign land.

A friend recently went to Cape Town, South Africa, and wanted to see the place where the two oceans—the Atlantic and the Indian Oceans—meet. He hired a guide who took him to Cape Point, where the supposed dividing line between the two vast bodies of water exists.

When they arrived at Cape Point after about an hour's drive from Cape Town, my friend looked out and saw a windy ocean with currents. My friend soon learned that in truth, oceans exchange water in many places, and there is debate over where the two oceans actually meet. Even if you were standing at an exact demarcation line, if such a line existed, it would still look like just ocean.

Seeing it for himself was an experience facilitated by the guide who knew just how to get there. Since my friend was on a business trip, this efficiency was welcome. "I love being a tourist," my friend told me, "especially for the first day. I try to set aside an extra day or two on either side of a business trip so I can be a tourist.

"I generally like it best at the end of my trip, after I've taken care of the business part. I am more relaxed then, and there is no stress because my meetings are over."

Finding the Right Guide

To find a guide, you can check with your hotel or travel agents, both at home and at your destination. It's usually best to set yourself up with an English-speaking guide before you go, especially if you want to be picked up at the airport and taken to your hotel. But don't hesitate to arrange for a guide once you get somewhere if you think you need or want one.

Major hotels are generally expert in finding the right type of guide for you. Usually one day in advance is enough notice, but two days is safer. If you decide at 11 a.m. to take an afternoon tour that same day, you might be lucky and find that a guide is available—but that is not the norm.

If your hotel has a concierge desk, that is the best place to ask for assistance. Otherwise, ask at the front desk. Hiring a private guide is surely a more expensive way to travel, but it can provide for a non-stressful type of trip, especially if you only have a short amount of time to sightsee in an unfamiliar place.

Tipping Etiquette in Other Cultures

- ✓ Americans are known worldwide for being good tippers. While some people think this makes us look foolish, I view it differently. If I can afford to give a few dollars or pesos or Euros to someone to show my appreciation, why not?

- ✓ One thing you'll notice is that many service workers don't wait around for a tip in other countries. I often have to say, "wait a minute," to get them to slow down. The smiles I get in return and the genuine "thanks" are all the reward I want.

- ✓ Know the currency conversion rate in whatever country you are visiting. Get small bills and coins for tips as soon as you enter the country. You don't want to undertip or overtip. Knowing what you are actually giving will keep you from giving the equivalent of a nickel or alternately a hundred dollars. In a pinch, you can always try handing out U.S. dollar bills.

✔ Tipping is actually discouraged in certain Asian countries such as Singapore. Knowing this in advance will make it easier for all concerned. When in doubt, make the gesture. But if it is refused, don't take offense. Remember, you are no longer in the United States.

✔ In many European countries, a gratuity is often added into the cost of meals and other services through a "service charge" or "cover charge." If you're feeling generous, you can always add a little extra, but this is discretionary.

✔ When hiring a guide or driver overseas, a generous tip or an appropriate gift is expected. It is also a good idea to give the guide and/or driver money for their lunch or dinner when you stop to have a meal. You don't need to have him or her join you, but it is a good idea to make sure the guide and/or driver has money for food. However, most guides will join you at meals if you extend the invitation. You should consider doing this as lunch or dinner is a good time to learn more about the place you are visiting. It is also a time when the guide will talk to you about where he or she lives, his or her family, and other usually interesting information.

Handshake Etiquette in Other Cultures

In the United States, shaking hands is something we do every day, and our handshake savvy can make or break us in an interview, business deal, friendship, or romance. Perfecting your style is an art akin to smiling and making eye contact. However, this custom varies across cultures, and it is important to recognize geographic differences.

✔ Americans tend to like their personal space more than Europeans. Thus our propensity is to shake hands instead of kissing cheeks like the French do on each side of the face.

✔ Among friends in Russia, a bear hug and cheek kissing are common, whereas in China, a nod or a bow is generally sufficient.

✔ In Japan, the traditional greeting is a bow. Though handshaking is common, it is usually done with a weak grip. Conversely, firm handshakes are *de rigueur* in Australia.

✔ In India, men shake hands with each other but may put their palms together and bow slightly when greeting a woman.

✔ Hawaii has a charming tradition of kissing. "Ha" is breath in Hawaiian and by kissing a greeting, you are getting close enough to share energy. That has evolved into a peck on the cheek for Westerners, though it is important to read the body language of a person as best you can. If you go to greet someone in Hawaii and that person stops and steps back, don't force it. The Hawaiian greeting actually evolved from touching noses, not mouths, to share breath and with the breath, share the spirit, or life force. That's a great concept.

Remembering Where You Are

After traveling to Hawaii, I immediately turned around and went to Texas on a business trip. I had just gotten used to the warm hugs and cheek kisses of the Hawaiians I met on the Big Island, and it took me a day or two to revert to comfortably shaking hands. But had I kissed strangers in Texas, they would have thought I was the "strange" one.

It's easy to pick up and adapt to other cultures. Just remember that you'll have to adapt back. Hopefully, you'll be able to retain the new ideas you've acquired, such as the Hawaiian concept of sharing life forces, even while you go back to your regular customs. Such as shaking hands.

Chapter 10

STAYING CONNECTED

Ahh . . . the cell phone, BlackBerry, iPod, newspaper, television, and laptop debate. With instantaneous communication, it's not as if we've gotten very far away even if we travel halfway around the globe. Or have we?

I laughed when a New York City cabbie told me that not all passengers talk to him. "Many of them are too busy on their Blueberries." (I swear, that's what he called them.) "They forget where they're going and tell me the wrong address. Then when we get to the wrong place, they get mad."

Tech Smart

If you intend to stay connected, and I'm not making a judgment one way or the other, make sure you know in advance what technology you need for the places you intend to go. Checking out related tech topics on the Internet is your best bet; with technology evolving and advancing so fast, it's best to get the latest information online. Call ahead or ask friends who have recently visited your destination, so you get firsthand advice too.

You should also think about the good and bad of staying connected, which is part philosophy and another part psychology. Children, spouses, parents, significant others, best friends, bosses, and clients all deserve our attention, and we have a responsibility to be reachable.

That said, being reachable is not the same as staying at home. The question is bound to arise as to how plugged or unplugged you intend to be. In this computer-addicted era, I feel a case of withdrawal coming on if I know I won't be online for even four hours. I read an article about a college professor who gave his students an assignment—for twenty-four hours, they could not use phones, computers, TVs, iPods, or any other electronic device.

Even during a power outage, we have battery-operated devices. Not to use any of them at all? Oh-my-gosh . . . it makes me nervous just to think about it.

I hate to be the one to break it to you, however, but you should know that once you are away, what seemed so vital from your office or kitchen table may, and I emphasize the "may," seem less urgent. Running out of suntan lotion on a catamaran in the Caribbean, or finding out that the pineapple you thought was safe to eat in Mexico City has been drenched in local stomach-bug-laden water to keep it looking fresh in the sun, can take on a high level of immediacy. Getting lost on a trail in the mountains or missing a subway stop in a busy city might take precedence over checking out the latest college basketball scores.

One of the benefits of traveling solo is that there are "no strings attached," that you are free to come and go as you please. Given that scenario, you might decide to make contact only once or twice a day. When I'm traveling, I keep my mobile phone turned on when practicable, but I may not check e-mail until late each night. It's totally up to you and your circumstances whether or not you choose to stay connected.

I got a kick out of a call from a friend while I was having breakfast outside in Palm Springs. My friend didn't know I was away and assumed that I was at home. I chatted away while waiting for my French toast to be served, happy to hear a friendly voice from home.

Other times I screen my calls when I'm somewhere new and exciting. If it's really important, the person will leave a message, and I can call back when I'm ready to switch from my travel mode to handling business or personal matters.

In a way, the technology revolution has helped make traveling alone less onerous. After all, with the right technology, we can answer the phone or respond to text messages and e-mail without other people knowing we're away. There's a great amount of freedom in that.

Of course, technology allows us to post an "I'm away without access to e-mail until next Tuesday" message, and to leave a similar outgoing voicemail. This always concerns me from a vulnerability standpoint. Just as you put a hold on mail and stop newspaper delivery to thwart potential thieves when you're away, it's a good idea to think twice before posting a universal "I'm away" e-mail. You may just prefer to keep your whereabouts private.

Time zones can be tricky, too. I live on the East Coast and was doing some writing work for a client in London when I got a travel writing assignment in Hawaii. The usual five-hour time difference between London and the East Coast had now become a ten-hour time difference. Luckily, the work did not require any conference calls that week, so I was able to balance both projects without complication.

The Basics

As a traveler, it is helpful to know how to find enticing activities, challenge yourself physically and emotionally, travel off-season to avoid crowds, and much more.

Increasingly, I am also growing more tech savvy as my traveling makes me ever more familiar with the gadgets and gizmos that keep us connected. With each hotel I visit having a slightly different set of instructions for using their in-room Internet connections, I am getting a forced education. I'm even finding it a challenge to learn more about technology rather than seeing it as the chore I once thought it to be. For me, this is like a new destination, and I am enjoying the journey.

Technology has transformed the travel industry in large and small ways. Long ago, I started making most of my reservations online. I like the control. In fact, I love the control. I can usually select the airline seat I want, the times I want, the airport I prefer, and a hotel rate that is acceptable in a location where I want to stay.

Technology is affecting the way we get around too. Old-fashioned paper maps and guidebooks are great, but they are being joined by PodGuides and handheld Global Positioning System (GPS) devices. WiFi (wireless fidelity or wireless Internet connection) enabled cafés and coffee shops are destinations in and of themselves. Often I plan my day so I can spend a bit of time somewhere checking e-mail and using the Internet. That may be in my hotel room, but increasingly it is more interesting to go to an Internet café or to use the WiFi in the hotel lobby.

As for the hotel itself, I usually choose one based on various criteria. Location and luxury must sometimes compete with a hotel's level of connectivity sophistication—wired or wireless and at what speed. Price is an issue too—is connection included as a guest accommodation, or is there a daily twenty-four-hour charge?

Basically, "staying connected" entails phone and e-mail service. Whether your family or office can reach you 24/7 will depend upon your activities and location. If you're climbing the Matterhorn in Zermatt, you won't be as connectable as if you were sipping a cup of coffee in Stockholm.

If you're only going to need it for a short time, you can usually use a public computer in a hotel or other business center. This usage is generally provided at a cost, but it is sometimes free. For security purposes, just be careful to learn to clear out whatever temporary files you create. I wouldn't recommend using credit card or similar information on one of these quasi-public computers either, also out of security concerns.

When you're traveling solo, designate one responsible person as your backup security detail. Leave a detailed itinerary with that person. If your travel plans change, make sure to convey your whereabouts to your security person. This is just in case something goes wrong. Odds are great that everything will be fine, but someone should know where you are in case you need some sort of assistance—financial, medical, legal, or even political.

Learning the Hard Way

On one of my trips to London, I thought I'd be smart and use a calling card from my hotel room to the United States. Not only did I get a calling card bill, which I expected, but the hotel charged me the equivalent of $400 U.S. This wasn't for long distance charges, just for use of the phone each minute of my outgoing calls even though I had used a toll-free access number. I would have been better off using my calling card from the pay phone outside, across the street from the hotel.

Alternately, international SIM cards can be obtained here or overseas, which would have allowed me to use my own mobile phone if I had a phone compatible with international bandwidths. A "SIM" card is simply a memory chip, or detachable smart card, that fits into your cell phone and carries your phone number as well as other identifying profile information. SIM stands for Subscriber Identity Module.

To work outside the U.S., a mobile phone has to be equipped with the frequency bands that are used internationally, which in many cases differ from those used in the United States and vary from carrier to carrier. Even if you happen to have a quad band mobile phone that works around the world, unless you activate international service through your carrier, or temporarily use a separate international SIM card, it may not work overseas.

It is also possible to purchase prepaid disposable cell phones in countries other than our own, or to rent a mobile phone that will work in other countries.

If you're traveling within the United States, it almost never pays to use domestic hotel phones. The charges are too high and erratic, and it is much easier to use your cell or smartphone, such as a BlackBerry.

The exception is if a friend or family member is calling to talk for a long period of time. If that happens, I'll sometimes ask the person to call back and go through the hotel switchboard, especially when cell phone reception is spotty in the guest rooms. Otherwise I may choose to go back downstairs, as cell reception is usually better in common areas like the lobby; but then I lose privacy. Receiving incoming calls through a hotel switchboard does not incur any hotel charges, so if the person I'm talking with doesn't mind, having that person call me back can be a viable option.

Advance preparation is always a good idea, especially if you're traveling overseas. Converters, chargers, add-ons to cell plans—it's best to be prepared if you need or want to stay connected.

The Night Before You Go
Never try something new the night before you go.

I made this mistake, and it cost me a night's sleep, not to mention tremendous angst.

I had decided to combine a business trip with some leisure fun, which is something I do often. In this case, I had a business conference in Los Angeles. Ahead of time, I flew to Palm Springs for a few days of R & R (rest and relaxation).

With one of my two laptops broken, I decided I'd better backup the one that was still working before I lugged it cross-country and risked heat, loss, theft, and technical difficulties with all my work on this one hard drive.

I went out and bought an external hard drive. The box was sealed, but there were no instructions inside. "How hard can this be?" I thought (foolishly as it turned out).

I proceeded to highlight everything on my desktop screen, which includes a lot of data files. Instead of putting everything under

"Documents," I have a bad habit of leaving current files right there on the screen where I can see them right away, just like all the pieces of paper sitting on my desk.

After I highlighted all the files, I must have told them to duplicate themselves. I intended to tell them to copy themselves onto my new external hard drive, but I did not communicate that properly. Suddenly, there was a duplicate of each file on my screen. I started deleting the duplicates. I would delete one and the computer would create two more. I would delete two and the computer started creating them faster than I could click.

Needless to say, I thought I had a computer virus. Ominous as that sounded, I sat up the night before my long trip, trying to beat the machine. *Never gonna happen.* But in my frustration, I tried. It was like playing a slot machine. My upcoming ten-day trip, which started early the next morning, loomed with my one working laptop out of commission.

I still took the laptop with me, as I really had little choice. This was a business trip, and I needed my files and my e-mail access, as well as a working computer so that I could meet upcoming deadlines.

When I checked into my hotel in the Palm Springs area, I asked at the front desk if the manager had any ideas. He had two—the tech guy at the hotel and a "computer geek company." Maybe I did something wrong when I called the computer company, but I could never reach a live person on the phone. Already upset about machines, I didn't want to talk into one. I just *knew* that I wanted a live human being to whom I could vent!

I took a nap and then went downstairs to speak with the concierge. I had not yet heard from the hotel's tech guy, and I asked if the concierge would contact him for me.

Back in my room, it only took a few minutes before I heard from "tech guy." He offered to come to my room to see the wayward computer, and we agreed on a time. When he got there, he listened to my tale of woe and then looked at the computer. I was prepared for the worst.

Within three minutes and a few keystrokes, he fixed the problem. I can't remember being that grateful to anyone for a long time. I offered him a handful of cash in thanks and was glad when he accepted it. Then we talked for about twenty minutes while he gave me several restaurant recommendations. I think he was trying to justify taking money from me by providing travel information, but I was just glad my computer problem was solved. As a result, I was able to relax and enjoy talking to him.

I was also able to enjoy looking out the window at the pool and the mountains on the edge of the resort where "tech guy" was telling me there were good hiking trails. However, I was merely anticipating the joy I would get from working on my laptop without the "slot machine" feature. I told you I'm computer-addicted.

Staying Unconnected

On several trips to Caribbean islands, the allure for me was the un-connectedness of my existence while there for a week or ten days. Barely seeing a newspaper, rarely getting or making calls, and staying off e-mail, I was subject to just the rumor and gossip of local events and concerns. No doubt the Caribbean has changed since I last visited, as the world gets ever-more connected. I've changed too—I'm more dependent on being reachable.

Still, it would be intriguing to have technology breaks, perhaps to wean myself off dependency on devices while reveling in snorkeling, sunbathing, shopping, rum punches, and dance clubs. I'm not sure I could do it anymore, but I'm willing to head back to the Caribbean any time just to test it (and because I adore the islands).

When You Absolutely Must Hook Up

To stay properly connected, three types of devices are most prominent—a mobile phone, a PDA or smartphone (such as a BlackBerry or an iPhone), and a laptop computer. You might also want to carry a pager, an iPod, a portable DVD player, digital camera, and other equipment. If you just need a laptop for sending and receiving e-mail, a device such as a BlackBerry or iPhone might do everything you'll need vis-à-vis phone calls and e-mail.

Keep in mind that however many devices you have, you'll need chargers, earphones, and protective cases. If you have a laptop, you'll need to pull it out every time you go through airport security. That's no biggie for road warriors who travel almost all the time on business. But for the rest of us, it's good to know what to expect in advance. Different vendors sell gadgets that will power and charge everything in one unit. If you need to carry a lot of different equipment, a combination power adapter might be an excellent investment.

Calling All Phones

Whether you're traveling in the U.S. or abroad, you'll want to have your own mobile phone with you. Even with potential roaming charges, mobile calls are less expensive than using hotel phones. I sometimes use a calling card purchased at Sam's Club; this works in the U.S., but it's important to make sure the hotel is not charging you for the 800 connection, otherwise this is not such a great idea.

> *Whether you're traveling in the U.S. or abroad, you'll want to have your own mobile phone with you.*

For using a mobile phone internationally, whether it is part of a PDA/smartphone or a separate cell phone, having quad service generally will allow you to use the phone here, there, and everywhere. This provides you with the ability to connect. Only a few U.S. service providers are adaptable internationally, however. Folks who travel and stay connected generally recommend you select a mobile carrier based on this criterion if you plan to do a lot of foreign travel. Even if your phone works outside the U.S., it is advisable to call your wireless carrier to price and implement an international plan in advance of an overseas trip; you should do this after you've determined your itinerary and the length of your stay.

You need to decide what's best and most economical for the traveling you'll be doing. If you're going only to one other country, you may want to get a SIM card for that country, as mentioned previously. Like a battery, you can replace your home country's SIM card with that of your visiting country, and then back again if you have the right type of phone and service. However, these cards may expire if not used within a certain time-frame, so you want to keep that in mind if you're only visiting sporadically.

If available, I personally think a throwaway (or disposable) phone purchased in a country where you're visiting is a great idea. You can buy a disposable phone charged with an appropriate amount of time, and then discard it when you leave. While there, you can usually add on more prepaid time as needed. If you're leaving the country, and there's still a decent amount of time left on a disposable cell, you can give the phone to a housekeeping staff member or taxi driver as an extra tip for good service. Some of these phones will also work back in the U.S. even though most U.S. phones do not work elsewhere.

Although you can rent a phone for international travel, if you're staying awhile, it's probably better to buy one or to get a new SIM card for use with your regular mobile phone.

Before your trip, it's also a good idea to go online and figure out area codes and country codes of your destinations, including the country exit code for calling back to the United States.

Laptops

If you want to bring your laptop along so you can browse the Internet for fun, play games, or watch videos, I advise you to leave the computer home and go out exploring instead. If you're bringing the laptop for work-related purposes and/or e-mail, that's okay. I still don't recommend that you stay in the hotel room using the computer as entertainment. That defeats the many purposes of traveling alone.

One of my friends tells me how he works on his laptop during flights and taxicab rides while on the road. If he's traveling with his wife, however, he avoids working in the taxi. This friend travels a great deal, so his working en route is understandable. However, for those of us who travel less, it's a good idea to pay attention to where we're going. After all, the ubiquitous computer will be there later. The drive into Johannesburg or Buenos Aires might be a once-in-a-lifetime experience.

In some countries with a lack of infrastructure, Internet service may only operate wirelessly (on WiFi). This can be true of an old hotel in Paris or a newer one in Dublin. Often a less expensive hotel property might have better connectivity than a luxurious one. In my experience, the room price does not always equate to technical efficiency, and I've found this to be true within the United States as well.

With a laptop, it is useful to know how to disconnect the wireless connection while you're in-flight or if you're somewhere with security concerns. You may also want to synchronize your computer so you can download e-mail from servers and automatically have access to them on the hard drive; doing this requires appropriate software. Once on the ground and back online, your e-mail responses would then automatically get transmitted around the world.

If you absolutely must have certain files or information with you, make sure to carry a thumb (or flash) drive with you that has duplicates of all important data from your laptop. If you're giving a speech and your presentation is on your laptop, you may want to take two backup thumb drives. If you have to use a different computer in an emergency, you'll be prepared with a few backups since thumb drives can get damaged, lost, or ruined.

A thumb drive has a memory chip, just like your hard drive, but it is wired differently. I sometimes e-mail my speech to myself as an e-mail attachment in addition to carrying a thumb drive. Worse case, I can always try to access it via e-mail if I have a technical problem with my computer hardware.

Even More Technology

If you're on the road a lot, you might consider getting VoIP, or Voice over Internet Protocol (such as Skype). This technology basically allows you to use your laptop as a phone, and it can save you a ton of money. Here's how it works: Whenever you connect your laptop to any kind of data stream, the phone is hooked up. Technically, your phone is thus traveling with you wherever you and your laptop go.

You'll need special software and a broadband connection to make this work, as well as an earpiece and microphone hookup. VoIP has a technology of its own, and it's not as good as cell phone technology for calls, but it is another option that can also incorporate e-mail and instant messaging (IMing).

Another form of Video Over Internet Protocol (VoIP) with streaming video will even let you catch the New York Rangers or any other team you follow, wherever you happen to be. Everything goes through an Internet pipeline, and the connections are good ones. Hooked into your laptop, this technology can make your computer a virtual satellite television system.

French Caresses

A friend of mine checked into a charming little hotel at a busy intersection in Paris. "My laptop crashed when I got there," she recalled. "I went to the desk and asked if they knew where I could take it.

"It was hilarious. The desk clerk pointed outside the door. Right across the street was this huge store—the French equivalent of Best Buy. 'How about there?' he asked.

"I went across the street with my laptop and went to the computer service desk. Two young French guys were there. The entire time I was at the service desk, they were caressing and massaging my computer.

"It was as if they were trying to convince me that they fully loved my computer. Only in Paris would someone rub a computer like that. But they couldn't fix it.

"Then I tried the Dell 800 line, but it was in French, and I don't speak French. I couldn't even pick the right extension.

"The desk clerk finally helped me get it going."

Online Slide Shows and Videos

Combinations of digital cameras, camcorders, and the Internet have created online shows available to everyone invited to the party.

Several services fill this niche, including photo and file sharing sites like Kodak and Flickr. Captioning can add a storyline or additional information when the photos are not self-explanatory, or when the photographer wants to further document the show. Video-sharing sites include Google Video and YouTube. You might want to read the fine print, however. Apparently some viewers think the posted material is free to them for other uses. As a result, legal rights are coming into question. Although you may be able to set privacy options and restrict those who can view your show, you run the risk of having your material used elsewhere.

A woman I know was traveling in India for several months. While there, she created and sent home several entertaining slide shows detailing her travels, which she posted online. They were a great way for her to share her travels with friends and family back home, especially since she was traveling on her own most of the time.

She was also able to upload short videos taken on a small camcorder. All she had to do was send the links home via e-mail to her friends and family, who could then access the videos. "They're not searchable," she wrote about her videos. "A lame attempt at privacy in a very public forum, so you have to access them from the link I'm sending you. Feel free to pass along, just not to creepy strangers."

So much for postcards and snail mail. The slide shows and videos made it back to the States weeks before her plane landed.

Chapter 11

DINING ON YOUR OWN

Some people dislike or even fear the idea of eating out alone, which can affect their decision to travel solo. Reactions range from being mildly uncomfortable to actively avoiding dining out alone.

One person told me, "Going to a restaurant or getting a drink alone is impossible for me. I'm hopeless. I can sightsee by myself or drive around by myself. It's not that I go hungry. But I'm so self-conscious—I eat really fast and then run away."

It's a mistake to let such qualms be a deterrent to enjoying yourself. Everyone is intimated by different things. But every time you conquer something that doesn't come easily, you will feel good about yourself.

I predict that those of you who are uncomfortable eating out by yourself will be glad once you've done it. In fact, you'll start looking forward to it. What's not to like? Good food? Being waited on? Satisfying your hunger and thirst in a unique place? Perhaps learning a few words in another language? Trying something you don't like and laughing about it later?

Not Another Bowl of Soup

Early in my writing career, I had the opportunity to write restaurant reviews. I remember having an assignment to write a feature story on the best places to eat soup. To meet the deadline, I went to three restaurants in one night and tasted two kinds of soup in each one. That translated into six bowls of soup in one night. I quickly decided that full-time food writing would make it too hard to stay thin.

By the third restaurant that night, I overcame any reticence I had to dining alone. After all, I had a mission, a reason to be there, and I had my figurative critic's hat on. I was busy analyzing the various restaurants based on service, ambiance, food quality, portion size, and the extra *je ne sais quoi* that makes a dining experience spectacular or not, or in this case, a bowl of soup warm and satisfying or not.

I was busy making notes and wondering the best way to compare tomato soup to chicken noodle. This left no time to be anxious over what anyone was thinking about seeing me alone. Or worrying that I wouldn't know the proper etiquette for sitting in a restaurant by myself. Or that I might run into someone I knew and be embarrassed that I was on my own. (You don't usually have to worry about seeing people you know if you're dining out of town or out of the country!)

If a maitre d' seated me in the back near a noisy kitchen, I didn't take it personally. After all, it merely affected the review I planned to write; so duly noted, their treating me badly would only hurt the restaurant. If the soup was cold, I would make note of that too or send it back. If they didn't react well to my complaint, that would also go in the review. Having a reason for dining out alone gave me courage to be assertive. And once "tasted," this assertion while dining out has become both a practice and a habit.

Planning Eases the Way

One of the best ways to approach eating out alone is to plan it, anticipating the pleasures and looking forward to the experience. After all, it is generally the unknown that most intimidates us. If we have an idea what to expect, that intimidation factor is greatly diminished.

If you know in advance where you're going to eat, get the address and learn how to get there. You can do this through the hotel concierge, by calling the restaurant, or by looking it up online and using mapquest.com or another search mechanism to get directions.

You can even check out the menu on the Internet and decide what you plan to order and how much you intend to spend. Plan in advance what you'll wear and what time you'll get there. By using this technique, many of the unknowns will become known.

Once you get used to dining out alone, of course, you'll find it much easier to "wing it." But for now, if you're hesitant, look into the details before you get to the restaurant, even if it's just quizzing the concierge before taking him or her up on a recommendation.

Advantages of Dining Alone
- ✔ You don't have to make small talk.
- ✔ You don't have to entertain anyone but yourself.

- ✔ You don't have to coerce a difficult companion to "make nice" to the waitstaff.
- ✔ You can splurge on expensive wine or champagne if you want.
- ✔ You can order a salad without explaining you're on a diet.
- ✔ You can order a decadent dessert without getting "the look."
- ✔ You get to choose the restaurant and the type of cuisine.
- ✔ You decide how long to sit there and whether to talk to other patrons or read a book.

Details Matter

Insist on a prominently placed table. Even if you were dining with someone else, you would hate being seated next to the kitchen, cash register, front door, or restrooms. If those are the only tables for one, leave and go somewhere else.

Consider dining at the bar if that option appeals to you. You really don't need anyone with you when you're sitting high up on a stool watching the activity behind the bar, whatever's on the television, or the comings and goings of the entire place.

One of my favorite friends invariably asks for a different table other than the first one offered to us whenever we dine out together. I laugh to myself every time as the host or hostess rushes around trying to satisfy him. My friend knows that where we sit makes a difference as to how much we will enjoy the experience.

I've learned from him, and from my experience as a restaurant critic, to pay attention to noise, the view, crowding, broken chairs, a table with a wobbly leg, crumbs, and any other details that may prove annoying. When I'm by myself, I notice these things even more because I'm not distracted by conversation.

I'm not advocating that you become difficult or annoying, just that you assert your need for a clean and comfortable place to eat. If something's wrong with the food—if they bring you the wrong order or your food is not cooked properly or tastes bad or the kitchen unexpectedly uses an ingredient to which you are allergic—by all means, speak up.

On a visit I took to France with a boyfriend, he ordered sausage in a restaurant near Versailles. Although it didn't taste right to him, he ate it anyway and became terribly ill. He refused to let me get him a doctor, but I'm sure he had a case of food poisoning. He recovered completely, but he lost a few days of our vacation during which time he was unable to leave the hotel room, with its proximity to the bathroom.

What to Avoid

I often avoid really elaborate, high-end, romantic restaurants when I'm by myself. These places are generally as much about the ambiance as the food. While you're certainly worth it and so am I, the service tends to be slow and the atmosphere can be the antithesis of comfortable for a solo diner. I've done it, and it's been fine, but if you're at all hesitant about dining alone, this is an advanced lesson that you should postpone until you learn to love eating out by yourself. It would be like a child painting a portrait before learning the difference between a circle and a square, or a music student playing a concerto before learning scales. You're better off easing into it.

Business Versus Pleasure

As in other aspects of traveling alone, some people are hesitant to treat themselves well because of an aspect of guilt. Perhaps they don't feel comfortable spending money on themselves, or maybe they don't feel it's appropriate to have fun without their spouse or significant other. But if it's during a business trip, they'll readily dine out by themselves.

Well, there's really little difference between eating out alone on a business trip and eating out alone on a pleasure trip. For some there might be a psychological difference—but the skills required are virtually the same. Only an artificial differential is at play. So go, eat, and enjoy.

A Skill You Already Have

Eating is something we all know how to do, and dining out is also part of our skill set. I'm sure that, at one time or another, you've been to a Starbucks or a deli by yourself and bought a coffee or soda or sandwich and consumed it without a companion by your side. Perhaps during lunchtime from work. Perhaps while shopping at the mall or waiting for new tires to be put on your car.

Just as you would not run a marathon the first time you went running, so too dining out evolves, and you get better at it the more you do it. Go. Have something delicious to eat, and remember to send me a psychic message of thanks. Indulge in a decadent dessert. Or have an entrée that's too complicated to fix at home like paella. (I've made it at home but it took me two days, so I order it out now whenever I have the opportunity.) This is not like learning to ski or snowboard for the first time. You already know how to eat, and you've been to restaurants. Only the "alone" part is new. So when you're in this situation, savor the food and the fact that you don't have to cook or clean up!

Techniques to Amuse Yourself

People watching is always a great sport and never more so than when dining alone. You can discreetly observe family dramas, couples who are into each other and other couples who are eating without talking, solo diners besides yourself, the restaurant staff, and in some places, such as in France, you can watch people with their dogs.

Other options:

- Reading a book or magazine—this is a good tactic between courses as long as you're not sitting in a dark restaurant trying to read by candlelight. Reading a newspaper is trickier, unless it's a tabloid or you have a large table.
- Writing—postcards or in your travel journal (described in detail elsewhere in this book).
- Sipping wine—I often order a glass of wine to slow down my meal when conversation might otherwise have done that.
- BlackBerry or laptop—checking e-mail or working on a computer is acceptable in many coffee shops and cybercafés. However, this is akin to eating at your desk at work. You're really not enjoying the restaurant scene and probably not paying much attention to the food or drink. I recommend signing off, at least for a little while.
- Listening in—eavesdropping on a conversation at a nearby table is okay if it doesn't hurt anyone. This is not polite to do if you're with someone else. But when you're by yourself, have fun. Just do this surreptitiously.

Places to Try

Not every restaurant is created equal. Depending upon your personality and where your travels take you, there are different types of places to try if you're hesitant to step out on your own, or even if you're not.

- ✔ *Sports bar*—you can watch one of the large screen TVs while chowing down on bar food and a beer. Everyone else will be watching the games too, and the camaraderie in a sports bar is contagious. You can cheer or boo for your favorite teams and get into discussions with strangers about stats and heroes.
- ✔ *Cooking class*—whether it's at Whole Foods' culinary kitchen in their Austin, Texas, headquarters or another venue such as a restaurant or cooking school, watching and/or helping to prepare the meal and then joining classmates in devouring it, is a great way of dining out with other people and yet alone. You can even attend a cooking school for a few days or a week, perhaps somewhere in the Italian countryside or on a Caribbean island.
- ✔ *Corner pub*—depending on the country you're visiting, these pubs are often lively, crowded, and generally welcoming.
- ✔ *Casino buffet*—you'll be so busy getting up to select your food that you're not likely to have time to be self-conscious.
- ✔ *Spa restaurant*—lots of people go to spas by themselves, whether it's a day spa or destination spa. In between getting a massage and sitting in the steam room or by the pool, you might want to get a bite to eat. Some spas serve food in their lounges or poolside; other spas have small restaurants. Most guests eat lunch in a robe, and most are there by themselves. Even if a guest came with someone, odds are that their friend or spouse is busy having a treatment while they are getting something to eat. Therefore, you won't be the only person eating alone.
- ✔ *Sports event*—it's easy to attend a ball game on your own. You can always enjoy a hot dog or slice of pizza in such a venue. While it's not dining out in a restaurant, it's not sitting alone in your hotel room either.

To Room Service or Not

The restaurant issue should not be viewed as a microcosm of the entire traveling alone experience. Issues may abound about what and where to eat, how to behave, what to spend, and more. If this continues to intimidate or worry you, or it just isn't fun for you even after you try it, there's always room service, carryout, a sandwich eaten in a park, or an evening group tour to a special restaurant or club. Just don't use this issue as a reason not to travel solo. There are ways to work around it.

I love room service breakfast. It gets me up and allows me to have breakfast in bed, to sip my hot tea while I'm getting dressed, and it saves time so I can get on with the activities of the day— sightseeing or snorkeling, shopping or skiing or whatever. However, for lunch or dinner, I like to get out and be served in a restaurant; or I buy a sandwich and eat it outside somewhere if the weather cooperates.

However, this is your solo trip, so you can do whatever you want. That's the beauty in all this.

What to Order

First, if you're allergic to something and you're traveling in a country where you don't speak the language or you don't speak it well enough, have someone write down an explanation of your food allergy in the local language. Then, as soon as you get to a restaurant, show the note to your waiter or waitress. (You might want to carry extra copies so you can give one to the server to take to the chef. Since you're in a restaurant setting, it's likely that your note will get wet or stained with food, so the extra copies will be useful.) Someone I know had "NO peanuts and bananas" written down for her in Thai by a concierge in Bangkok. It saved a lot of problems.

That said, next you should experiment a little. A steak is a steak is a steak. But Mexican food in Texas is different from what you find on the East Coast. If you're actually in Mexico, it's even more remarkable. One of the charms of traveling is the unique nature of the cuisine. While you may not like something you order, it's certainly more interesting than just playing it safe and ordering as if you were back home.

Still, stay within your comfort zone until you get tempted by those profiteroles served at the table next to you in a Parisian café, or . . . (you fill in the blank next time you take a trip somewhere).

Invite Others to Join You

If you're at a business conference during the day, with evenings left to your own devices, consider asking a fellow attendee to join you at dinner. If you're taking a ski lesson or riding a ski lift up the mountain with someone else, perhaps he or she would like to join you for an après ski drink or appetizers, if not for a complete dinner. Be receptive to invitations from others too.

If another person declines, however, don't take it personally. Maybe they're just shy, have other plans, or perhaps they truly relish dining alone. If the other person accepts, be prepared to be bored or charmed—it can go either way. But don't be fearful of taking chances, either alone or with others. Dining out is an enjoyable activity, and it's a shame to miss out on culinary delights in new places. Then again, maybe you'd rather save the time, money, and calories. Just make sure to get the proper sustenance.

Making It an Adventure

A woman I know grew up in New York City. She travels extensively for work and is often on the road solo. When I asked about her experiences, she immediately responded, "I love looking at the sights. But more than that, I love tasting the coffee and biscotti in every city.

"No aspersions on Starbucks or anything," she continued. "But I always search for a local bake shop where I can walk around and absorb everything and see how it's different from what we have back in New York."

Truth:

Being part of a couple or crowd does not necessarily make you more comfortable. In the right setting, among strangers, you can truly learn to love your own company, to savor a meal, a glass of wine, to even linger over coffee or espresso and perhaps a few biscotti, and leave satisfied with both the food and the experience.

Chapter 12

THE BEST STORIES

Perfect days, fantastic excursions, clear weather, and delicious food are all great. We can certainly strive for such ideal circumstances when we travel. More than likely though, the times you will remember and the stories you will tell, stem from those moments when things didn't go exactly as you had planned or expected.

When Things Go Wrong

An executive from a large corporation told me this story:

"On a trip to San Antonio, I was told to keep all the windows and doors shut. It was during the floods, and there were crickets everywhere. I was in my room sleeping with a bunch of crickets. The noise was loud, and they were flying and jumping everywhere. At least they looked like they were flying.

"Because it was raining a lot, there were more of them than usual. They would fall on your shoulder, hair, back, even into your purse. And you'd have all these crickets all over you. The locals know to shake—it's a habit for them.

"Well, I didn't know I was supposed to shake, and when I went into a restaurant, suddenly people were staring at these critters all over me."

Airport Difficulties

The same executive had another tale to tell from a lunchtime flight out of LAX Airport in Los Angeles:

"I got to the airport early so I could buy some lunch. I ordered, but the man behind the food counter refused to give me a sandwich the way I wanted it. I told him that I would like a different kind of bread. All I wanted was a breakfast sandwich with ham and egg on sour dough. Usually they do it on a croissant, but I wanted sour dough. They had the sour dough for another kind of sandwich, so I knew they had the ingredients.

"'No, we don't do it like that,' the man said.

"I kept asking, and he kept telling me, 'No.' Finally, a woman who works there told me she would make it the way I wanted.

"Before all that trouble started with my sandwich, I went to check in at the elite line because I qualified. I waited and waited and finally asked the guy when he would get to me. I thought he was going to kill me. All he said was, 'Take it or leave it, lady.' He just left me standing there.

"After about a half hour, I finally had to go wait in the regular line. It's tough at the airport."

All Time Favorites

I always find it interesting to ask busy people about their mini-escapes—the weekend getaways or the one-day or one-afternoon excursions. Sometimes these short trips have to satisfy a traveler's need to get away, so they'd better be good.

Here are a few I've heard:
- ✔ "My soul is tied to Nags Head. It's not very glamorous, but it's the truthful answer. I go by myself in the wintertime when I need spiritual time alone."
- ✔ "We're never the same after going. That's why I go somewhere every weekend I can. Afterward, I can't wait to go the next time and bring back a little of the world."
- ✔ "My dream is to be on a boat going from Key West up the coast, stopping at all the keys and tiki bars and not connected to the Internet or a cell phone. I settle for short trips with my cell phone on all the time. One of these days, I'll make it."
- ✔ "I take the bus to Atlantic City. It costs $28, and they give you a voucher for $20 worth of coins once you get there. So the trip costs $8. You arrive at noon. By the time you cash in the voucher, get something to eat and play the slots, five hours goes by pretty quickly. Then you're back on the bus by 5:30."

A Hop, Skip, and Jump—Across the Pond

I got a chance to fly to London, spend forty-eight hours there, and fly back. I agreed to go, but I thought it was too short a trip to go such a long way.

I mentioned my plans to a friend. She told me that she's flown from the U.S. to London twice, but never stayed overnight.

"On your way somewhere else?" I asked. I previously had an

eight-hour layover at Heathrow; I took the train into the city for lunch, and then went back to Heathrow in plenty of time for my flight to Nice on the French Riviera.

"No," she answered. "The first time I went, a boyfriend flew me over with him on the Concorde. It was noisy and the seats were uncomfortable, but it only took two and a half hours from New York. We saw my boyfriend's sister's new baby, ate dinner, and then flew back.

"Another time, a friend convinced me to fly over on British Air, spend the day shopping at Harrods, and then fly back again at the end of the day. We slept on the plane."

"What did you buy?" I wanted to know.

"A bookmark—it was all I could afford at the time. My friend bought a lot of clothes."

My forty-eight-hour trip to London was a long one by these standards. And my friend and I are not the only ones to take short trips overseas. Another woman I know did the same thing—she went to London for a weekend to visit a friend. At the time, she was in college and she didn't tell her parents. But now that she is married with two children, she remembers the adventure fondly.

As Wayne Gretzky, the famous ice hockey player, is always quoted as saying, "*You miss 100 percent of the shots you never take.*" In travel language, that means you should not miss out on opportunities. Even if the getaways are short, they no doubt will be memorable—if for no other reason than that they were so short!

Climbing Up Is Often Easier Than Coming Back Down

When I visited Mexico City, I took a bus to the Pyramids at Teotihuacan (pronounced tay'-uh-tee'-wah-kahn), which is where the Pyramid of the Sun is near the Pyramid of the Moon. Adventurous person that I am, I decided to climb up the face of the Pyramid of the Moon rather than just standing around at the base and visiting the gift shop.

Except I had a problem because the steps are small and time-worn slippery, and I wear a size ten shoe. There are no railings either, so I quickly realized that walking up a series of steps made centuries ago for people with smaller feet was not to be. But I was there already, and I really wanted to climb the pyramid. After all, I might never get another chance. I was there and the pyramid was there.

So, I got down on my hands and knees and crawled up the pyramid. When I reached the top, I was able to stand up, and I was thrilled that I had made it. Then suddenly a hailstorm started. Can you believe my luck? The hailstones were large and hurt when they hit. It was cool but not cold, though of course I didn't know what to expect from the weather patterns in Mexico. Perhaps my slow and inelegant crawl up the face of the pyramid had disturbed the ancient pre-Aztec spirits, and they were determined to inflict revenge.

In any case, I decided to get back down to the base as quickly as I could since the hailstorm was showing no signs of letting up. However, walking down without a railing and with normal-sized feet that were bigger than the tiny slippery steps seemed too daunting a task. I was scared because I could not figure out how I was going to make it back down. I even tried to go backwards on my hands and knees, but that was a no-starter too. There was no way I could get back down the same way I had gotten up.

Luckily a man named Jorge came along and offered his assistance in a halting mixture of English and Spanish. I readily accepted his offer (not that I had any other choice) and I held onto him for dear life. He wanted nothing from me once we reached the bottom—not even my thanks. He merely slipped away, having saved me from the hail and my fear of falling down the face of the pyramid, which looked much higher and more formidable from the top than it did from the bottom.

Sometimes You Outsmart Yourself

Flying in coach can leave a lot to be desired. The flight attendants sell snacks instead of feeding you substantive food, and you are cramped into ever-smaller spaces for ever-longer periods of time, especially if a gate isn't ready upon landing or there's a queue for flights ready to take off. As a result, getting upgraded can be delightfully pleasant. You're well fed, you have somewhat unlimited alcohol if you are so inclined, and there's more room in larger seats that often recline. You can even tuck yourself in with the comfortable pillows and blankets provided.

Usually other passengers are nice, whether you are traveling in coach, first, or business class. But prior to boarding on an upgraded ticket recently, I had a premonition that I might regret requesting an upgrade on that particular flight. In spite of my foreboding, I accepted the upgrade. As it turned out, I was unprepared for "Her Royal Highness," as I now refer to the woman who sat beside me. She impatiently tapped her foot while I stowed my carry-on in the overhead compartment. In an annoyed fashion, she kind of moved (about an inch) out of my way when I said, "Excuse me," on my way past her aisle seat to my window one.

I attempted a few pleasantries but she didn't respond. Okay, she didn't want to talk—I could respect that. But the problem began after dinner when I needed to use the restroom. With her seat completely reclined, the woman next to me was completely blocking my way. I politely asked her to move and she impolitely ignored me. I asked again. "You can get out," she told me, motioning for me to climb over her.

Earlier that evening during an airport layover, I had a wonderful visit with some fellow journalists who had been on a trip with me that week. They teased me and gave me examples of how I had let other people on the trip get away with more than they should. From the conversation, I learned something about myself. Although I am outgoing and friendly, I sometimes get timid when confronted with a bully.

Now that I had it pointed out to me, I was determined to make sure it didn't happen again. I refused to climb over the snooty lady until she moved her legs out of the way. She should have stood up, but that wasn't going to happen in this lifetime, not without coercion.

I proceeded to the first-class restroom. On the way, I spoke to the purser, who told me she was the head flight attendant. I complained that I should not have to climb over the woman and risk falling if the plane suddenly careened due to turbulence. The purser acknowledged that the woman next to me was difficult, which had been apparent when the woman ordered the many drinks she was consuming.

Back after my bathroom break, the woman had her heavy first-class blanket on the floor where I needed to walk. I asked her to move it, and once again, she refused. I stood my ground, not wanting to fall, and she finally moved it a few inches. The woman was on her fifth or sixth drink at this point. Just my luck. You'd think that with all that drinking she'd need to go use the restroom herself, but during the entire eight-hour flight, she never got up. Buoyed by the encouragement of my newfound travel-writer buddies, I was determined to stand strong.

Unfortunately, my heart was pounding, adrenaline coursing through my blood vessels preparing me for the fight-or-flight response, when she got yet another glass of red wine and put it on the narrow console between our seats. I mentioned to the flight attendant—a different one from the purser—that I was afraid I'd knock over the wine while I slept during the long night flight. The flight attendant recommended to the woman that she use her tray table instead of the console so I wouldn't knock it over.

The minute the flight attendant left, the woman said, "I'm sure the idiot would." She also proceeded to call me other names, which I choose not to repeat.

"Excuse me," I said. She ignored me. I know that sticks and stones . . . but I was determined to stop the bully. I buzzed for a flight attendant and told the purser, when she arrived, that the woman was calling me names. The purser proceeded to tell us that since I had requested an upgrade, if we had an altercation, I would be the one forced to move back to coach.

On my next and only other trip to the restroom that flight, I had to buzz for the flight attendant when my neighbor once again refused to even acknowledge my request for her to move her seat down so I could get by. The flight attendant came, the woman started to move her seat, and then the moment the flight attendant walked away, my unfriendly neighbor halted the seat, which was now only partially out of the way. I managed to get by, and then I went to talk to the purser again.

I asked for her name and she started to get nervous. I told her I didn't appreciate being told that I'm a second-class citizen here in first class and if I fell because I had to climb over the woman next to me, I would hold everyone responsible. I told the purser that I respected her authority, but I didn't believe she was handling the situation well by catering to this woman when her behavior was denying me access to the aisle.

I also told the purser that she needed to stand by our seats until the woman completely moved the reclined seat when I needed to get up, because otherwise the snooty lady only moved the seat part way. The purser promised to talk with the woman, who finally stood up and got out of her seat when I returned. "Thank you," I said because I knew what standing up had cost her, but she looked through me as if I hadn't spoken.

I tell this tale of the flying princess, but it is in direct opposition to most of the excellent conversations I've had with strangers on planes, trains, and boats. The kindnesses, the friendliness, the minutes and hours shared in chance meetings that enrich me when they occur, are wonderful.

Unfortunately, if you put yourself out there, you'll also run into some bad apples.

The purser didn't know that I'm a travel writer and I chose not to tell her. She only knew that I had requested an upgrade and was therefore, in her world, a second-class citizen. When I got off the plane, I told a gate attendant what the purser had said about the upgrade. "That's the dumbest thing I've ever heard," he said immediately, soothing my injured feelings and reassuring me that the trouble was just a flight attendant with poor judgment who had not handled a problem well.

I encourage other travelers to speak up, politely but firmly, because nobody deserves to be pushed around.

I encourage other travelers to speak up, politely but firmly, because nobody deserves to be pushed around.

Standing Up to Bullies

When I was a little girl of about five, the other kids on our suburban neighborhood block picked on me. Many of them were a year older than me; at that age, that meant they were also bigger. My parents were really loving, affectionate people. Maybe some of the other kids in the neighborhood were not as lucky as I was, but many were older, bigger, *and* tougher.

One day, two of the kids started a fight with me. My dad happened to be home, so it was probably a Saturday. He knew that if he stopped the fight, they would just pick on me next time. Instead, he told the two six year olds—a boy and a girl—that I would fight them, but one at a time instead of letting them gang up on me. "Leslie will fight you," he said, "but it's going to be a fair fight."

I proceeded to beat up the boy. He was older and bigger than me, but he was a bit of a sissy. Then my mom came outside. Instead of her stopping the fight, she brought me a banana to eat for energy. I ate the banana, and then I proceeded to beat up the girl who was one of the toughest kids in the neighborhood and who had a mean streak. Neither kid picked on me for at least a year after that. So I learned early on that standing up to bullies is the only way to stop them. I'm still surprised that my parents let their little girl fight, but they each had a lot of backbone and were probably trying to instill that in me.

Life can be tricky, however, and situations are no longer as simple as a tussle between little kids in the backyard. Still, the principle is the same—you can't let bullies get away with pushing you around. While I fondly and frequently tell the story of my parents and the banana fight, over the years I'd forgotten the message behind it.

Thanks to my fellow journalists and our three-hour airport layover, I was reminded of this life lesson. I used it with the flight attendant and the snooty lady. And I plan to use it on other travels if necessary.

Recently, when I had a complaint, an officer manager told me my complaint was valid. "As long as someone is not doing something just because they like to get their way," the office manager said, "it's appropriate to complain."

Something or someone in the universe seems to be sending me this message. I am passing it on.

Credit Cards, Cash, and Cabs

A friend, who happens to work for American Express, told me this tale:

"Whenever I get into a taxi, I look to see if they have a sticker that says they accept the card. I also asked recently when I was on a business trip. The taxi driver nodded, acknowledging that he did accept it.

"But when we got to my destination, he said that he would not accept it. I said, 'I told you that I planned to use my credit card.'

"At first, he continued to insist that he would not take it. Then he finally said that I could use it but he'd have to charge me more.

"I'm the wrong person to tell you're not accepting the American Express card."

Since hearing my friend's story, I'm looking forward to the day when plastic is more widely accepted by cab drivers.

Although I never personally charge a taxi fare, I do always use a credit card when I'm going somewhere and using a car service. In various places, a car service costs about the same price, or just a little more than, a taxi for the same route. The convenience of using a credit card for the fare and the tip sometimes swings my decision to select the car service.

Be aware, however, that some car services keep a portion of any charged tips. So if you want to make sure the driver gets the entire gratuity, it is best to hand him a cash tip.

Hidden Alley

A Texas business associate agrees with me that, "Sometimes the worst experience makes the greatest story."

She recalled the time she was on a train that arrived in Vienna at 2 a.m. With her backpack in tow, she looked for her hostel from 2 a.m. to 4 a.m. "I walked by the alley where it was located so many times," she told me. "I just didn't see it. The address didn't seem to exist. Finally I figured out where it was.

"I'm so glad that happened because now I know I can make it. The thing to remember when traveling alone is that you have nightmares, but then you make it through. It keeps things in perspective.

"What a cool experience, after all. Not many people can say they've seen the back alleys of Vienna at 4 in the morning. Now that it's over, it doesn't seem that bad."

Weighing Turtles

A woman I know encouraged her husband to go off to Italy by himself to take a cooking course, as cooking is one of his passions.

When it came time for her turn, she chose to join an Earthwatch expedition on the island of St. Croix in the Caribbean. "It was a way for me to break into solo travel without totally winging it," she said.

As part of a group of ten volunteers and two leaders, she helped in a conservation project to protect the nesting sites of giant endangered leatherback sea turtles. "We counted the eggs and moved the nests if they were too close to the tide because the salt water would kill them. There are fewer nesting beaches for the turtles to choose from worldwide, so they sometimes leave the nests too close to the ocean."

They also measured and weighed turtles that came up on the beach. "We used a tripod contraption with slings." she explained.

The expedition was always at night. "We walked ten to twelve miles a night on the sand, carrying flashlights. It was exhausting, but it was also so beautiful on the beach at 3 a.m. I would never have gone out walking in the middle of the night by myself."

Working together on the sea turtle project was a group of men and women—no couples, no friends—all solo adventurers. Similar types of group tours, some less strenuous, can be found through university alumni associations, museums, religious groups, and a variety of volunteer projects.

"All these vacations are a good way for people to stick a toe in the solo travel waters," she said. She and her husband travel together too. "The longer we stay married, the more we want to try an occasional separate adventure," she said. "With this group, I did exactly what I wanted to do—no compromising with traveling companions. I got to walk on the beach all night long. It was my dream and my fantasy."

"Short" Story

Another woman I met bragged to me about how she traveled through southern Italy in the heat of the summer. "My husband wanted to wear shorts, but I insisted that he had to look proper at all times by wearing long pants and a dress shirt. I didn't want to be embarrassed in front of the well-dressed Europeans even though it *was* really hot."

"Do you travel together often?" I asked innocently.

"He divorced me right after we got back," she answered. She seemed surprised. I wasn't.

Notre Dame

A friend spent two days in Paris on her way to a business meeting in Europe. "You know what my life is like," she told me. "I'm overcommitted, always juggling lives and schedules.

"To get on a plane and be totally on my own schedule, especially as a mother, is a wonderful feeling. With my kids out of school, summer does not have as many pressures. My family relies on me, but on the other hand, when you're traveling, there's little you can do about it.

"It's great to step out and go someplace wonderful like Paris—to have this fabulous city in front of you. It felt completely selfish to sit in a café for two hours watching people, and to wander around taking in the city.

"It was no big huge thing—just wandering. It started to rain, and I went into Notre Dame. I listened to the service. I could appreciate the beauty of the cathedral while I waited out the rain. It doesn't matter what religion you are.

"The best part is eating when you want and sleeping when you want. As long as I was going to Europe, it made sense to tack on a few extra days. The whole thing was wonderful—I really had a good time. It reminded me that I need to go more often.

"This trip is a mini-version of what I'd like to be able to do. I told myself that after my children are grown, I'm going to get an apartment and spend six months in Paris.

"That would be real luxury—to drop out of my life for a few months. That would be real indulgence."

Thought: Travel can give you lots of retrospective stories to tell, adding completeness to a trip. If you are traveling alone, these funny, annoying, and poignant episodes are the ones you share with others and the ones you remember long after the trip is over.

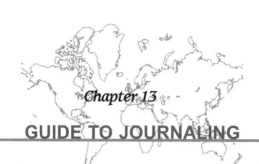

GUIDE TO JOURNALING

Journaling is the process of writing down thoughts and feelings. It can enhance self-discovery and understanding. Writing is also an effective way to deal with startling or stressful feelings.

Most of us want to change something about ourselves—whether it's losing weight, advancing our career, or improving a personal relationship. Journaling assists people in the process of self-change. It is a creative tool that gives people an opportunity to sort out their reality. It fosters a form of self-talk that generates awareness.

Journaling during travel is a creative tool for all of the usual self-discovery reasons. It's also a way to mark where we've been and fix it on paper so we can return to read about our exploits long after our memories have faded, or after those reflections have changed, as often happens.

As a professional writer, I write constantly. I'm always trying to figure out how to incorporate my notes into an article, a speech, a story, or a book. Journaling is not something I need to consciously do. I've trained myself to be self-aware on paper and on a computer screen.

For non-writers, journaling may not seem natural at first. However, once you get used to doing it, I predict that you'll love it.

The Medium Not the Message

I have finally convinced myself to write freely in beautiful journals, on beautiful paper, to feel that my writing is worth the expensive books that I have been collecting for years—to accord my musings and thoughts the proper forum for recording them.

You can find beautiful journals in stationery and bookstores, in gift shops, and at spas. You can also use a child's black and white schoolbook or a little notepad that fits neatly into your pocket. Even a collection of paper napkins acquired at the many restaurants and bars in which you find sustenance can do. No one is judging you, and you shouldn't judge yourself. Cross out something if you are so inclined, or turn the page and start fresh.

One way of journaling while traveling is to write a series of postcards or e-mails to a particular special person. You need not send the messages, or you can send them off but still keep copies. I find that writing as if speaking to someone else facilitates my own journaling. Perhaps it offers a safer distance to my internal journey; perhaps it is just a writer's trick that I've learned.

Years ago, I asked a successful published author how he dealt with writer's block. "I just start writing," he told me. "I write, 'the door opened,' or whatever. It doesn't matter. You can throw out the beginning later. Once you start, you'll be fine. There need not be any such thing as writer's block." His advice has kept me in good form all these years. When I teach writing workshops, I dispense his advice to the participants. I have found it to be true.

Different Kinds of Journals

For me, writing is a passion, but it is still work. When I want to journal while traveling, I tend to do so in a more visually artistic medium. My mom did this by collecting matchbooks wherever we went together on a mother-daughter trip to Europe.

One way of journaling while traveling is to write a series of postcards or e-mails to a particular special person.

My brother does this through his photojournalism. His poignant photos help tell the tale of his journeys.

I sometimes collect menus. Not all restaurants are thrilled about that, but I find that if I ask to take the menu without its expensive outer folder, they will usually give me the inserts or provide miniature copies they have created for just such a purpose.

Another type of journal is a collection of postcards from a trip. I sometimes buy them just for my collection. I don't generally write on them, but I could if I wanted to record my thoughts. If I need to send a postcard to someone, I buy two of the same one if I like it enough so I can keep one in my "journal."

Don't misunderstand, I am constantly writing while I am traveling. It's just that for me, it is usually about stories I want to tell readers, not about introspection. That's an occupational hazard for me that most journal writers don't have to face.

I heard Nora Ephron, the screenwriter, speak at a luncheon. She said her mother, also a writer, told her and her sisters that, "Everything is material." That's true for a professional writer, and it's just as true for a journal-"ist."

Journal Themes

There are different kinds of books. Fiction, for instance, includes various genres like mysteries and romances, thrillers, science fiction, and even sub-genres such as historical romances and detective thrillers.

In nonfiction, it is the same—there are biographies, history, cookbooks, gardening books, science, nature, politics, sports, even that great category—travel.

We all have varied interests and read different kinds of books. But then we each have our favorites too.

I'm not suggesting that you view your journal as a book project. It should not take up a lot of your travel time. But it should document your trip in some way, shadow it, as it were, reflect your thoughts or your steps or your evolution or your wonder.

What I am suggesting is that you write whatever you want, in whatever form it takes. Don't worry about how it's going to turn out. This is not homework, this is not a work assignment. It is not for anyone else but you to read unless you decide to share it later. You're already planning, or thinking about, traveling alone. Keeping some sort of journal is just a document to help you express some aspect of that travel.

It can be in the form of notes:

"Today, I saw part of the Vatican's vast art collection."

"After two days, we finally spotted one of the few surviving Royal Bengal Tigers in this part of India."

"Had a great lunch on St. Barts—grilled lobster at an outdoor restaurant on the beach."

"Found gorgeous hand-painted scarves on the *Rue de Rivoli*."

"Thought about my job and realize that I need to make a change."

"Spoke with a friendly couple from Toronto. We're going to compare notes in the lobby after dinner tonight."

A Food Journal

If you like to cook, and you're traveling to a new city or region, you might write down all the different dishes you try. Like this:

Monday—a panino (grilled sandwich on Italian bread) from a vendor's stall at the train station.

Thursday—handmade dark chocolates at the hotel when I arrived.

Saturday—wandered around the open-air market. Saw the most beautiful mushrooms. Didn't recognize what kind.

Or you can collect business cards at each of the restaurants you visit and jot notes on them as to the date and perhaps the meal you order. If you are a wine aficionado, this is a good way to keep track of whatever vintages you drink.

A Meditation Journal

While you're traveling on a train, having your morning coffee, or sitting on a beach watching the seagulls, jot down your thoughts— random or otherwise. This can be written in stream of consciousness or in a more structured manner. You can be wordy or succinct.

You don't have to do yoga or traditional meditation to transfer your meditative ideas onto paper. While you are writing, if you want to make a list of all the gifts you need to buy before you go home, so what? If you want to write down all the home improvement projects that you want to accomplish in the next year, do that.

You'll find that no matter what is on your mind, once you commit it to paper, you'll feel just a tad lighter psychologically, and more emotionally ready to tackle the issue or project.

Or you may just be more ready to get on with a seemingly frivolous day of sightseeing, museum touring, or white-water rafting— without the issue of the gifts or a new garage door opener invading your enjoyment of the here and now. Not that I believe any travel activities are frivolous. Whether entertaining or educational, stimulating or relaxing, whatever activities you choose to do or pass up while traveling help create the fabric that you're weaving for you and you alone.

Keeping a journal of your random thoughts or worries may assist you in learning something about yourself, or deeper meanings may remain elusive. Later you can go back and read what you wrote, and it will no doubt be clearer. For now, you just want to jot down your notes.

An Activities Journal

Monday—took bus to Bath and wandered around the former Roman ruins.

Tuesday—bought a beautiful onyx ring on the *Ponte Vecchio.*

Wednesday—watched a rugby match at a pub with the locals.

Thursday—took a tango lesson.

Friday—saw penguins in their natural habitat as the cruise ship neared Antarctica.

(The above activities would not be from any one trip. They are just examples.)

A Doodle Journal

This one should be self-explanatory. I wouldn't try this one myself, because I tend to doodle geometric shapes over and over. My artistic geometry is relaxing, but it wouldn't say much about my internal or external travels when I got home.

Some people can draw cartoons or funny faces, or even bits of buildings or other scenery. For these people, keeping a doodle journal would be great fun and perhaps very revealing. Or not. It just might be therapeutic. Again, this is a personal journey—it doesn't need to be a work of art.

A Spiritual Journal

This is between you and whomever or whatever you believe, whether that is God or nature or the special bond that exists between many of us as we share this fabulous world of which you are getting to see a new piece that will hopefully illuminate more of it for you.

A spiritual journal can include a list of names from markers in an historic cemetery, your reaction upon taking a tour of the Cathedral of Strasbourg, a series of thoughts while you sit on a patio outside your room in Santa Margherita Ligure. It can be what comes to mind while viewing majestic elephants on safari in Kenya's Amboseli National Park, it can be your feelings having just reached the summit of Mt. Kilimanjaro or at the end of the day hiking in the Australian outback.

This can be a list of promises to yourself, a list of things for which you are grateful, or a list of questions for which you are seeking answers. It can be written on a bus winding through the Andes or in downtown Los Angeles. It can be written in an airport terminal or on a deserted beach. It can be written at night or early in the morning. Or not at all.

A Shopping Journal

This is not meant to be a shopping list (although that's okay too). It might be notations of favorite shops or items you find in a Moroccan bazaar, or gemstones used in the Native American jewelry on sale at a New Mexican pueblo or outside the Palace of the Governors in Santa Fe. It can be a list of purchases made on the *Rue du Faubourg Saint-Honoré* or in London's Harrods department store.

It can be of items you purchased or items you saw that were too expensive to buy. With a digital camera, it can be easy to document jewelry or handcrafts. Or you can keep a list of recommended stores for friends back home when they are ready to travel.

One of my favorite shops in Florence is a particular leather store that sells beautiful handmade leather boxes. Whenever you find a personal favorite, you might want to jot it down for future reference.

A Reading Journal

A friend of mine, who loves to read, finds that between work and family and the regular activities of day-to-day life, she doesn't have more than a half hour before bed to read on a daily basis. On extended travel, however, she'll read as many as ten or twelve books.

A recent conversation with her about her love of mysteries gave me the idea for a reading journal—an ongoing one to keep track, for no particular reason, of each book she reads while she is traveling, and how what she reads may or may not be influenced by, or influence her enjoyment of, that particular journey. Such a reading journal would parallel her travel journey; it could be really interesting.

A Legacy

I suggested earlier that e-mails, postcards, or letters can be a form of journaling. After my parents passed away, I was left to be my dad's executor. (My mother predeceased him.) This turned out to be both a chore and a blessing. It fell to me to go through my parents' papers.

My dad was always a great writer. In fact, he wanted to do that for a living but the vicissitudes of life led him on a different path. He spoke about writing with great fondness, though, throughout his life. It is no accident that both my brother and I have become writers, in effect living out his dream. Dad imbued us with the belief that words on paper, or spoken in a play, or captured in a song, are priceless.

In going through all the many papers my parents left behind, documenting financial ups and downs, birthday cards treasured from when we were kids, recipes, and much, much more, I found a series of letters my dad wrote to my mom when he traveled alone on business to Chicago, Pittsburgh, and Cleveland for his job with the B & O Railroad. He was never gone long and didn't travel often, but he took those occasions to write to my mom about how much he missed her, what he thought her views of the city he was visiting would be, and his activities for that day, including who he ate dinner with, what he ate, and what it cost.

This travelogue, which I've found now that they are both gone, is a glimpse into his mind and his thoughts, as well as the relationship he had with my mother. To me it is both fascinating and bittersweet. I almost feel that I am intruding, though it is more a record of everyday interactions than intimate thoughts. Still, it is somehow personal, especially when he signs off telling her how greatly she is missed, even while he is gone just a few days. My dad trusted me and my judgment, so I am the keeper of his travel journal, of sorts, which happens to be in the form of letters.

When my mother died, I wanted more than anything to find a series of letters that she would have perhaps left to me for all my upcoming birthdays. I would have opened them only one year at a time. One of the things I missed most was her handwriting at the bottom of a letter or card, telling me that she loved me. I would have given anything to find such a cache of love, bundled together and waiting for me.

I have yet to finish going through all my parents' papers, but so far, those letters are not to be. However, my mom kept a small travel journal when she and I took a trip together to Europe. And she kept notes about another one of our trips together to St. Thomas. I have these musings of hers, to treasure along with my dad's letters.

When we were in London together, my mom wrote this in a little black "Travel Log" she took along: "Piccadilly Theatre. Saw a new show called *Metropolis* through Harrods' ticket agency. It was very good—but had to change seats three different times due to smoke, an unusually large head and a broken seat. Nevertheless—enjoyed the evening."

The smoke to which my mom referred was from the stage effects.

With our seats close to the stage, the smoke from the stage production got in our eyes. I had forgotten about it until I reread her entry for that night.

Then a few days later, Mom wrote: "Took a taxi from our hotel to Her Majesties Theatre where we saw *Phantom of the Opera* after a quick lunch at McDonald's. We had first row center seats and saw and felt everything firsthand."

We actually felt the spit when the lead sang his part, we were so close to the stage. Between the smoke of *Metropolis* and the spit of *Phantom*, our theater trips were rather eventful.

Guarding Your Secrets

Now that you've been journaling through a visit to other places or lands or cultures, you should take care of your writing. Whatever you think of your creation, keep in mind it is a work in progress. You can share it with others if you decide to do so later, but you don't want to risk losing it.

Whatever you do, be careful NOT to put your journal in checked luggage. If lost, you can replace shoes, but not your thoughts as captured day to day. Besides, if you have the journal with you, a plane presents a wonderful opportunity for noting how annoying that person is behind you who keeps kicking the back of your seat, or grabs hold of your seat to pull himself up, waking you or otherwise disturbing you, even grabbing your hair, in the process.

> *Whatever you think of your creation, keep in mind it is a work in progress.*

As a writer, I never pack my note-books in checked luggage because my notes are my work product as well as my joy. Treat your travel journals in the same way. Trust me on this. They form a part of your memory of the travel and as such, they are invaluable.

The Importance of Frequency

It doesn't matter how often you write in your journal. This isn't a diary. This isn't a command performance. There are no rules. You can write in your journal once, twice, even five times a day. Or you can skip a few days, a few months, or just pull it out when you're traveling once a year. You can do it on one trip and never do it again. Or it might satisfy you in some undefined way so that it becomes an ongoing pursuit. Journaling is not meant to be a chore, but a joy. It can be done if you're dining alone—that's a good time to catch up with yourself. Or not. It's up to you. You can retire your journal or make it a lifelong habit. This is for the internal you. It can become a seductive addiction—this pull towards writing. Or you may find it fulfills a need at one stage of your life, for one or two acts, and then you don't need it anymore.

Maybe you jot down recipe ideas and use the journal as a self-devised cookbook, where you write down cooking and gardening ideas you get in other places and other countries, then add in notes when you try to duplicate the ideas in your own kitchen or backyard.

Writing Hints (or Prompts)
Sit down in a café or coffee shop and open your journal. Write your name. Write where you are and where you are going.

Q. What do you want to see?

Q. What most excites you about this journey?

Q. Is there something you'd rather not be doing?

Q. Why is that?

Q. Can you get out of it? Or make it better? (Like slipping out of a meeting a little early and walking around the city; only do this if you won't be reprimanded for being absent. Or surreptitiously write in your journal during the meeting, unless, of course, you're the speaker.)

Prompt: List the Top Ten things you most want to do. (If you just want to sit on the beach and read a novel for ten days, write that down. The best answer is what you really, truly want to do. Remember, this journal is just for you.)

Prompt: If money were no object, how would this trip be different? (I like to pretend I've won the lottery and plan how I would spend the money. Playing this game turns me into a winner, as I get to know what I really want to do. Then I find a way to do it even without winning the lottery.)

In London several years ago, I saw a wonderful example of my fantasy on a theatrical stage. I got to see the very funny *Spend Spend Spend*, which was a show about that very thing—winning the lottery. It tickled my funny bone. More importantly, it shows that I'm not the only one who likes to fantasize.

Of course, not all my fantasies are about money.

Travel is a chance to live out your fantasies. A journal is one way of recording it for your own amusement later on. If you decide to share it with others, you can do that too. Or not.

Just remember when you get old that you need to leave someone in charge whom you trust to know what to do with these journals of yours. If you become famous, this may be even more important.

In the book, *The Bridges of Madison County*, the character Francesca Johnson leaves behind a journal that reveals a love affair with a man other than her husband. The journal is found after her death. I'm sure this is a case of fiction mirroring real life, for this must have happened to someone somewhere. Or more than one someone in several some places.

Prompt: "The door opened and there I was in (fill in the blank)."

Thought: Perhaps a blank page in a travel journal is as exciting as an upcoming trip. One doesn't know what will appear there. The anticipation of unknown treasures looms brightly, beckoning the adventurer on.

Chapter 14
MEMORIES THAT NEVER END

We cherish special travel memories forever. Nothing can take them away. They become part of who we know ourselves to be.

For those of us who travel extensively, memory triggers are useful tools for bringing back those "ah-hah" moments that we possibly forgot, or that slipped our minds.

The definition of the French word, *souvenir*, is one of memory, remembrance, and recollection—to occur to the mind.

Souvenirs can take many forms, and as I've said before, there are no rules. When it comes to solo travel, there is no one to remind you that a sunset looks similar to one shared on a beach in Fiji, or that the volcano that is erupting was dormant when you last visited. Thus souvenirs are important for solo travelers.

Any keepsake or memento will do—a photo, airline or theater ticket, subway or train receipt, snow globe, shot glass, journal entry, a brand of Swiss chocolates bought twice a year, a pair of chopsticks, a watch bought in Hong Kong or Singapore, a stuffed kangaroo—use your imagination and wanderings to find "souvenirs" that remind you of something you saw or thought or felt.

Luckily, there will be other times when a slight breeze, a sound, a whiff of perfume, a story on an evening newscast or morning show, a flower, a phrase, or some other serendipitous stimulus will remind us of our travels. Savor each of these moments and smile whenever you experience one.

Nostalgia

Walking up Broadway in New York City recently, I thought, as I always do when in Manhattan, of my mom who grew up in several of the five boroughs and always spoke fondly of New York. It is her nostalgia that I enjoy, mixed with my own memories of her that make me miss her.

I came across several stores devoted to selling buttons, beads, and other decorative items such as tiaras and metal appliqués. My maternal grandfather was a dress designer, and he worked in the

New York fashion industry. When my grandfather designed women's fashions for the New York garment industry, times were tough. There was money sometimes, and sometimes not.

My mother's inheritance from my grandfather included heavy glass apothecary jars, with tight fitting glass lids, filled with layers upon layers of colorful and variable sized buttons—buttons of many kinds.

I never knew my mother's father because he died a month before I was born. Now that my mother is gone too, I have possession of the button collection. I guard these jars as if they contained diamonds instead of plastic buttons because my mother treasured them, and so they are meaningful to me.

Walking in New York City, I am drawn into my mother's memories through the many stories she told. In my mind, I am both in the present and, for just a moment, in the past. It is a kind of time travel that crosses three generations, as I walk along hoping to blend in, not to attract too much attention, in this big, noisy, exciting place.

Little Bars of Soap

One of my favorite episodes of the TV sitcom *Friends* has Ross taking bottles of shampoo and conditioner, bars of soap, even a Bible from a hotel room. In the lobby as he is leaving, his suitcase drops and falls open. Talk about embarrassing!

I confess that I also used to be guilty of taking soap and shampoo. I've stopped taking the shampoo and conditioner, but sometimes I do still take the little soaps. I love the soaps, especially when they are high-end French soaps. I really enjoy using them when I get home.

I stopped taking all the other stuff for several reasons. Sometimes it spills. If I only have a carry-on bag when I'm flying, I'm limited to the amount of liquid I can carry. Mostly I stopped because years later, I had all these little bottles in my linen closet with almost no room left for sheets and towels. Then I had to clean them out. One way of minimizing the clutter is not to collect it in the first place.

One of my friends, who travels everywhere on business, collects all the shampoos, conditioners, and lotions; when she gets home, she donates them to homeless shelters. That's a good idea.

I'm reminded of a trip I took with a former boyfriend. We checked into a hotel, and I went to use the bathroom. When I came out, I told him there was no soap. "We should call and ask them to bring us some," I said innocently.

"There was soap. I put it in my suitcase to take home," he said. "But we only just checked in five minutes ago," I laughed. "Could I have one bar to use while we're here?"

Ironically, that man was pretty generous, he just had this Ross-like quirk.

Chianti

I am a wine drinker, but by no means a wine connoisseur. Still, I have personal tastes and preferences. I tend to like red wine, usually a somewhat dry Merlot or Cabernet.

On one of my trips to Florence, I sat at an outdoor café and tried to order a glass of red wine. "I'll bring you Chianti," the waiter said.

"No, thank you," I answered. "I don't like Chianti. What else can you bring me?"

"I want to bring you Chianti."

Thinking he didn't understand my English, I tried again. "I really don't like Chianti."

"This Chianti is nothing like what you get in the United States," the waiter told me knowingly. "What we ship to the United States, we feed to our pigs. What we drink here is different. Trust me," he insisted, walking away. He wasn't giving me a choice, and it was only a glass of wine, after all.

The Chianti he served to me turned out to be wonderful. I laugh to this day anytime I think about drinking a particular wine from another country. I wonder if this is wine they prepare for an American audience, or if this is what they drink themselves. If anyone offers me Chianti while I'm in the United States, I generally turn it down—with a smile on my face. If I'm in Italy, I readily accept. Perhaps such safeguarding of the best wines for the home markets is why, in France and Italy, table wines are usually pretty good.

After the Chianti in Florence episode, I took a wine tour of Alsace, France. Alsace is a region apart from Lorraine. When you study the two regions in high school, they are always paired together for these areas of France alternated, historically, between being part of France and being part of Germany.

At any rate, Alsatian wines are generally white. Again, I am not a connoisseur but some of my fellow tour mates were wine experts. I watched while they tasted and spit—which is what you are supposed to do. I sipped and swallowed. It's not that I wanted to drink a lot, it's just that spitting in a communal bowl was unappealing to me.

I was fascinated, however, by how the wines are processed and put into barrels to be bottled later. We stood in a vast underground storage facility with many, many barrels of wine. The proprietress broke out a special bottle of Gewurztraminer—a sweet wine often served for dessert. I had previously tried it on the tour and didn't like it. But this particular bottle of wine was absolutely fabulous.

Apparently, the grapes used for this one wine only survive every few years on one side of a particular hill. They bottle the very limited amount of wine in half bottles, since the winery can only produce a little of this precious treat. Tasting that wine was worth the entire weeklong trip. I will never forget it. No one was spitting that one out either.

When in Rome . . .

. . . do as the Romans do. This goes for the rest of the world as well.

I attended a bullfight in Mexico City. People ask me, "How could you stand the blood and gore, knowing that the bull would be killed?"

The bullfight took place in a huge stadium, and I was way up toward the top. I was so far away from the field, which looked tiny from my perspective, that it was almost like watching it on television, only on television I would have had a better view. I remember the vendors hawking giant Hershey bars, and I felt, somehow, as if I were at a football game.

The event was interesting to me because no matter what the sport, and I use that term loosely because I know an animal was killed, sports events are exciting. And my curiosity got the better of me. Many of the places I've visited and lots of the things I've tried were the result of unending curiosity.

The bullfight is not something I feel the need to repeat, but I'm glad I went. I vividly remember the crowds of people, the meal I ate at a stand out on the street before entering the stadium, and the feeling of being somewhere different that was oddly just the same.

Photographs

One of my friends has a photo of himself taken at the top of Mt.

Kilimanjaro; it is framed and mounted on the wall in his office.

I have a framed photo of myself in a ski jacket in downtown Aspen and another of myself all dressed up and ready to go out on the town in Monaco. As it turned out, the casino where I went in Monaco was pretty deserted. I later learned that the best places to go in that small country are by invitation only. I was all dressed up with nowhere to go, as I had no private invitations. Still, I have a photo I enjoy, one that causes me to laugh to myself for getting all dressed up for nothing.

Some of the best travel memories are those in which we laugh at ourselves. Going alone, we need not try to posture, pretend, or impress. Our own views of ourselves are important, of course. But laughter certainly increases endorphins, those pleasure sending and seeking chemicals that keep us in good spirits. Who better than to laugh at ourselves, to take ourselves a bit less seriously, to recognize the humor in situations rather than getting angry or frustrated?

Some of the best travel memories are those in which we laugh at ourselves. Going alone, we need not try to posture, pretend, or impress.

Perhaps that is the best lesson of travel, for the more we know about this world of ours, the more we understand the people in it and how it evolves. As a result, the more we laugh, the more we can take life in stride.

Besides using skill when taking photos, the trick to successfully enjoying your travel photography may be defined by your determination to label and organize the photos. Digital photography makes this much easier. It helps to keep in mind that what you know and remember will change over time. Dates and place names are important to record; capture specific details relevant to the images too.

It's a great idea to pick out one or two favorite photos for enlarging and framing. You can look at them on a regular basis and if not laugh, at least evoke a smile or two and generate some endorphins.

Before You Take That Photo

I remember taking photos of indigenous people in Mexico City and having them throw nuts at me. (They were sitting on blankets selling the nuts.) As mentioned earlier, I subsequently learned that in some cultures, taking a person's photo is equivalent to stealing their spirit. Now if I'm in doubt, I'll ask. If I can't communicate because of a difference in language, I'll motion to my camera. If they shake their heads no, I abstain from taking the shot. No photo is worth hurting someone that way.

At the Pueblo of Taos in northern New Mexico, some of the Native Americans were okay with having their photo taken if you gave them a few dollars, while others were still uncomfortable with the entire process. It warrants repeating that I hope the ones who readily smiled for my camera after receiving a tip didn't believe I was taking something from them.

Unless you're a professional photographer, keep camera equipment small and lightweight. I always travel with spare camera batteries (subject to flight restrictions), and now that I've switched from film to digital, it's easy to carry extra flash memory cards too. You can buy batteries and memory cards while traveling, but they are usually more expensive in places that have a lot of travelers. The memory cards take up such a small amount of space that it makes sense to bring along extra capacity.

I tend to take more photos when I'm by myself—perhaps because I have a bit more leisure, perhaps because I have the desire to share what I'm seeing with someone back home, perhaps because I notice more as I am looking around rather than at a companion. Still, the best part about taking photos on a solo trip is looking at them yourself later.

It's almost always a good idea to ask someone to take your photo in front of the Taj Mahal or Eiffel Tower. If the potential photographer doesn't speak your language, just point to your camera and to yourself. There's a sort of universal language about asking others to take your photo. The only time this isn't a good idea is in a really poor area where the person to whom you hand your camera might run away with it. If the area is that bad, you're better off taking a group tour anyway; in that situation, you can ask someone in the group to take the shot.

Toll Booths

On one of our road trips when I was a kid, my mom drove for a while to give my dad a break. We came upon a toll booth. My mom threw a quarter and missed. She opened her door to retrieve it and realized that other people had missed too, but most had merely thrown in another quarter and driven away. Mom got out of the car and started collecting the wayward quarters, until my dad yelled at her to get back in the car before the police came. Then he laughed about her antics for the rest of the afternoon.

We never pulled up to a toll booth after that without remarking about Mom's partnering . . . I think it was with the Commonwealth of Massachusetts. I still think of that every time I throw change into metal containers on toll roads.

A close friend of mine took a road trip with her family. She was driving while her husband took a nap. Along the way, she stopped and threw money into a toll machine. Her young son didn't say anything until later when her husband awoke. "Daddy," the little boy confided incredulously, "Mommy threw money out the window when you were asleep." It always makes my friend laugh too.

Watching Movies and Reading Books

One of my trips to Italy included a visit to the Vatican. Since then, a new Pope has been chosen, and as I watched the coverage on television, I related more than I had previously to Saint Peter's Square. As I read *The Da Vinci Code* and *Angels and Demons*, I felt special connections to the room at the Louvre, in Paris, where the Mona Lisa resides and to places within the Vatican.

In New York City, the Empire State Building, the Plaza Hotel, Tiffany's, the Statue of Liberty, and many other landmarks are regularly featured in numerous films. Sites in Washington, DC, are often used for filming too. To those familiar with the nation's capital, even a shopping excursion to Georgetown Park Mall can bring to mind at least one film chase scene.

Many worldwide points of interest are depicted in films and described in books—far too many to mention. The ones I've referenced here are just a tiny portion of those that have triggered the imaginations of authors and filmmakers.

How wonderful when sitting up late at night reading a gripping novel to be able to reminisce about having been to the very spot described on the pages in front of you. Or while watching a movie on DVD or cable—it's great to see a site you once visited play an integral part in the plot.

A good author can make a reader feel as if he or she is actually in a place that is described. A good traveler adds his or her own experiences to the author's descriptions, and the result is an enhanced read. A book is always seen through two sets of eyes—the writer's and the reader's; the richer the understanding by each, the better the experience.

With films, there is an analogous relationship, this time between the director's eyes and those of the viewer's. Travel sharpens our eyes—whether they are those of a reader's or viewer's, thus making enjoyment of subsequent entertainment infinitely more satisfying.

All Good Things Must End

After returning home from our travels, some of us experience a letdown. Although we may be ready to return to the familiar and the ordinary, the excitement of our travels is over for now. Meeting new people, practicing language skills, having someone else make the bed, dining out in restaurants, hiking through a forest, and discovering a bird or flower previously unknown to you—all the adventures are over, at least temporarily.

We face piled-up mail, which we've wisely had held by a friend or the post office until our return; e-mails and voicemails that we may have accessed while away but for which we deferred responses; necessary home repairs as minor as lawn cutting or snow removal but demanding nonetheless; family responsibilities; even exercise classes. We may need to buy milk and fruit and other perishable food and cook it ourselves. We probably need to do at least one load of laundry to wash our travel clothes. We have to go back to work.

One person I know calls this "returning to reality." I don't exactly agree because traveling is real too, but I understand what she means and suspect that many people feel the way she does.

Gone are the little luxuries of days without regular chores. Gone are the experiences of swimming with dolphins, kayaking, viewing sunsets over the ocean or waterfalls hidden in forests.

The weather might have been gloomy while we were away, but we knew we could always slip into a bookstore or café, stay inside our hotel room and order room service, or take a walk in the rain or snow, marveling at the fact that we could let our hair get messed up, or our clothes get wet, and it didn't matter. We were not on the way to the office or to an important appointment. We just were.

It is possible that life while traveling is better, more fun, more people-oriented or more secluded (depending on your lifestyle), than when you're at home. It is even possible that life at home is better but you still need change and variability—a need that is best met by leaving home for a time.

The feeling of loss—of a good time, of relaxation, or of excitement—is exacerbated when you travel by yourself. Invariably, if you have one or more traveling companions, someone has gotten on your nerves at least once. There's no such annoyance when you're by yourself, nothing to make you glad even just a tiny bit that the experience is over.

The very act of solo travel is immensely satisfying, as you invariably conquer a fear or insecurity.

The very act of solo travel is immensely satisfying, as you invariably conquer a fear or insecurity. After all, there's no one else along to drive across the bridge or to choose which path to follow. No one else is around to consult about a restaurant selection. There are concierges and guidebooks, of course, and taxi drivers too, but no one else has a vested interest in your having as good a time as you do unless they are going along.

The act of solo travel also entails internal journeys, where we learn something about ourselves or try out a behavior that exists somewhere deep inside us but which we've never before allowed to surface. We might find we like being a bit more solitary or perhaps funnier or more athletic than we thought. Maybe we are introspective and traveling alone allows us the freedom to recognize a new desire, a fantasy, or an interest that we wish to pursue.

When it's over, we experience a loss even though we retain whatever we've seen or learned in our memories. But the loss is real.

This too shall pass. Just as you had to return home, so too you'll be glad to be back. It may take a few hours or even days, but a moment will come when you're back in your groove, when your luggage is unpacked and put away, when you've got fresh bread and milk in the fridge, and a pot of stew on the stove that is fabulously familiar in place of a dish you've never before tried. Everything has its place, and now you're back in the home place.

Still, the slightly sad, slightly depressed state of mind that exists when you wish you were still on the road or in the sky or on the beach, or whatever, is not fun. If your family or friends or co-workers make a fuss at being glad to have you back, this sadness may be ameliorated. If it's quiet at home or the office, or if someone ignores the fact that you were gone and acts as usual, or if there are immediate demands placed upon you, you might long for the days when you were still traveling.

This is a natural process. Years ago, someone wise told me that life is not a choice between good and bad. If that were so, decision-making would be easy. Instead, life is a choice between various options that all have positive and negative aspects. So it is with going places and coming home.

There are a few things you can do to make the transition easier and more palatable:

- ✔ Text, call, or e-mail a friend with how you're feeling. Hopefully, he or she is empathetic enough to respond back right away.
- ✔ Tell someone a story or anecdote from your recent travels, thus perpetuating the trip through the telling of a highlight or humorous event.
- ✔ Engage someone in a discussion of travel—sharing what you just experienced and listening to something they've done in the past.
- ✔ Order pizza or Chinese food delivered and get in bed with a good book your first night back.
- ✔ Look back by reviewing your digital photos (thankfully, we are no longer dependent on getting film processed, which took time).
- ✔ Best of all—look forward and start to anticipate the next trip even if it's as far off as a year. Looking forward almost never "trips" you up.
- ✔ Know that the travel you just completed will never be over because you will carry it with you always. Memories may fade, souvenirs get broken or discarded, and you may forget the details, but the experience is now part of your make-up, part of your personality, and a portion of your knowledge base. Nothing can take it away from you. You may forget the exact experience, but you are forever changed, influenced, and bettered by having challenged yourself through exposure to a new piece of the world.

Telling Stories

The act of "telling a story" connotes imagination and prevarication. While storytelling is an art that is best enjoyed with a little exaggeration and drama thrown in for good measure, the best stories are often the ones that actually happened while also being the ones that nobody completely believes. These are not "fish" stories, but rather recitations of incidents—funny or poignant or frightening—that occurred in our travels.

These anecdotes can be short or long, shared verbally or in writing, by phone or at a party, but travel makes interesting stories and sparks the telling of similar stories by those in your audience. In the telling, you encapsulate the nuggets of your experience in a way that preserves them. The great thing about traveling alone is that only you get to decide which nuggets to relate and share, and which ones to keep for yourself. You may want to keep almost all of it for yourself, or not. That's up to you.

If you're a little down when you get home, share at least one anecdote with someone. You'll feel better, and you'll intrigue whomever you tell. Then give the other person or persons a chance to tell stories if they so choose, even if those stories are from way in the past. The real charm of knowing fellow travelers is in the swapping of tales.

"Once you have traveled, the voyage never ends, but is played out over and over again in the quietest chambers, that the mind can never break off from the journey."
—Pat Conroy, *The Prince of Tides*

Chapter 15

THE NEXT TRIP ON THE HORIZON

I'm generally a happy person. I like people, I love my work as a writer, and I can amuse myself through reading, walking, sports, and other activities. So I was surprised recently when I was rather down one day, though I shouldn't be surprised because even those of us who are usually happy have our moments. My consulting business was going particularly well, and I was busy, maybe a little too busy.

One of the airlines sent me an e-mail about a fare sale. Like every good procrastinator, I stopped what I was doing and read the e-mail. I'd been wanting to visit Lake Austin Spa Resort for a while. I liked the fact that it's small, they teach kayaking, I have the chef's cookbook and find its dishes tempting, and it was bound to be a different kind of jaunt from my other trips to spas in Arizona, Florida, and California.

Though I loved those previous spa trips, the hills and lakes of Texas seemed to offer something different, which is what travel, in my opinion, should be about. The people who vacation in the same place every year are vacationers. That's a marvelous thing to be, but it is distinct from travelers even if the vacationers have to travel to get to their destinations.

Busy as I was, I stopped what I was doing and booked a few days at the spa. Then I called some places in the city of Austin, adding three days onto my trip with plans to stay at the venerable Driskill Hotel in downtown Austin.

As I got excited about learning to dance the Texas two-step and learning to play Texas Hold 'Em poker, my mood elevated immediately. While I had various things to look forward to at home, I realized that I am genuinely happier when I have a trip in front of me—something with a bit of the unknown to challenge and excite me.

I went back to writing an article for a client, found a speech I had written to forward to another client, and reveled in my upcoming six-day adventure to Austin. I remembered that the University of Texas is there, and that the city is known for its live music and vibrancy. I was particularly happy that the spa resort offers kayaking if the weather is not too cold, because kayaking is something I've always wanted to try.

I also vowed that the next time I'm just a little bit down, I'll look into what's around the bend or across the globe. I know now that I need to look forward to seeing a new place or trying a new sport. Maybe I don't need it as much as oxygen and water, food and affection. But it's in my soul—a learned behavior that is part of my emotional make-up and that lifts my spirit.

I also vowed that the next time I'm just a little bit down, I'll look into what's around the bend or across the globe.

Travel has become a sort of healthy compulsion because it keeps me stimulated and interested, and hopefully interesting. But that's not why I do it. I do it because it makes me happy. Planning, preparing, and taking a trip just might make you happy too. If there is no available traveling companion, don't let that prevent you from traveling. Just choose your destination and make it happen.

My Love of Travel

When I was young, I had not seen that much of the world, experienced that many new places, or tried that many new things. On a tour boat at New Hampshire's Lake Winnipesaukee, I fell in love . . . with travel. Other loves have come and gone, but I've loved travel ever since.

During that same trip through New England, my family stopped to ask someone for directions, and we were told that our hotel was "a spit up the road." I've never heard that expression before or since, but I'll never forget it. It was colorful, and it stayed with me.

Recently on the Big Island of Hawaii, I asked for directions and was told to drive ten minutes and then turn right. "Is there a light or a road sign when I get there?" I asked.

"No," I was told. "It's just a ten-minute drive." Not quite a spit up the road, but similar. That's one of the great values of travel—context.

Paying the Price

No matter how much you love to travel, it is not a good idea to spend more than you can afford. Even if you get to walk on the Great

Wall, even if you get to see kangaroos or elephants in the wild, if the trip is going to cause financial problems, rethink it. Instead of flying to Hawaii for a week on the beach, if you don't have the funds, stay home and take day trips in the car, or maybe plan an overnight trip to somewhere nearby with a clean but inexpensive hotel.

Then, if you absolutely feel the need to buy a souvenir or to eat out in a nice restaurant, you will have the money.

An advantage of solo travel is that you can spend money when you want or cut corners when you want. You can take the subway instead of hiring a driver and town car or eat a take-out sandwich instead of a five-course sit-down meal. You can splurge; but you don't have to do it all the time.

If money is a concern, one way to pay for your next trip is to save regularly and in advance. Open a separate savings account and put money into it each paycheck. Try to put the same amount in each week or pay period, whether that's $50 or $100, so it becomes a habit. You will be surprised how quickly the money adds up. You might be able to take the next trip sooner than you thought or take a bigger trip than you originally planned.

Just make sure to leave something in the account for your next trip. Don't ever close the account, and you will always find your next travel experience just around the bend.

Vacationing in Place

This past summer I tried to "vacation in place." I had the money to go somewhere but I wanted to stay home and try the pretense of spending a week as if I were on the road.

I adore tennis. During the Grand Slams, I keep my television tuned to matches day and night. I've also gone in person to the U.S. Open in Flushing Meadows (Queens, New York) and had a "grand" time. But it can be expensive going to New York City, staying in a hotel, eating out in restaurants, and buying tournament tickets.

I knew I was writing this book, and I knew I planned to recommend "vacationing in place." But I'd never actually tried it myself—not for more than a day or two.

Living in an area that has a professional men's tennis tournament leading up to the U.S. Open, I usually attend one or two matches each year. This summer I got a weeklong pass and planned to go to the matches every day on my own, without friends in tow. I would sleep at home every night and eat meals on the tournament grounds during the day.

It was great. I actually had less stress than if I had gone somewhere, because I got to sleep in my own bed and shower in my own bathroom. I had none of the hassles of travel, but all the adventure of attending an event both day and night, meeting new people who share my intense interest in tennis, being entertained, and eating all my meals out. Yet the expense was minimal. At night, I did check my e-mail and voicemail, but I do that even when I'm away.

> *You don't really have to go anywhere, you could stay home . . . so you challenge the travel gods, "Okay, make me an offer I can't refuse."*

Sometime in the near future, I would like to attend the other Grand Slams—Wimbledon with its strawberries and cream, the French Open at Roland Garros, and the Australian Open.

Despite my wanderlust, I wouldn't hesitate to travel in place again, and I recommend that everyone try it. It does not replace traveling to other places, but it certainly augments it. Find something that appeals to you, as tennis does to me, and just do it.

If you're used to traveling with someone and your circumstances have recently changed, this will ease you into traveling solo. I predict that you will have so much fun, you'll quickly plan a trip much further away. Even if that's not the case, this is one way of identifying activities and events you truly love. To enjoy a week close to home with enthusiasm, and without all the distractions of being in a new place, it's almost a must that your chosen activity or activities be ones about which you are totally passionate.

Winging It

Spontaneity, flexibility, adaptability. . . whatever you want to call it. You've got a few days or a week of plans that get changed or cancelled. Your boss tells you you're entitled to vacation time that you'll lose unless you take it right away. A family event gets postponed. A trip with a friend or spouse or lover gets cancelled due to that person's work commitments or a fight between the two of you. You're a consultant who finishes a project early with a few days of time on your hands. Your kids are away at sleepover camp. Whatever. Life throws you a curve ball. This is the perfect time to check out last-minute, cut-rate fares that the airlines love to send via weekly e-mail. If you want to take a cruise, a last-minute booking can be much less expensive. After all, you don't care where you're going. This type of spontaneity is cost driven, rather than destination driven. You want value. You want the best deal possible. You don't really have to go anywhere, you could stay home . . . so you challenge the travel gods, "Okay, make me an offer I can't refuse."

Of course, you want a clean hotel room in a safe area, but you don't need butler service or an in-room massage. Or maybe time is more precious to you than cost—so you *can* arrange for touches of luxury. This kind of last-minute winging it tests your mettle. It dares you to be adventurous. You are unprepared, for you've not had time to study guidebooks and maps, query friends and co-workers, or do exhaustive research on the ubiquitous google.com.

The trick to last-minute travel is advance organization. As mentioned before, the road warriors, those men and women who travel from consulting project to consulting project across the country and the globe, always have their overnight bags half packed. Leisure travelers can do the same. Just make sure to have handy a set of chargers for your cell phone and laptop, a T-shirt for sleeping or running, athletic shoes, and any prescription items you might need.

Include an extra lightweight collapsible suitcase so that you can buy things on the road and expand out from your luggage. With advance organization, you can pack in a few minutes and then catch a cab to the airport, or throw the bag into the trunk of your car and hit the road.

I always try to keep a nearly full tank of gas in my car and get the tire pressure checked regularly, so that my car is in proper form to head out on the spur of the moment. In an emergency, this would be a good thing. For fun, this is also a good thing. Bottled water, some cash, a pair of jeans, an umbrella, and a rain jacket are all useful items to have close at hand for a car trip.

Cash Comes in Handy

A few years ago, I thought I could outrun a blizzard. I was traveling back from an out-of-town trip on a route that normally takes an hour.

After two hours of harrowing driving, I finally saw a gas station about a half hour from my home. I pulled in, parked my car, and knew immediately that I would not drive anymore that night. I had witnessed several accidents, and I couldn't see more than a foot ahead.

I went inside the convenience store part of the gas station and told the attendant my plight. He let me use the restroom, and then he generously gave me his chair to sit on, telling me to relax. Not long afterward, a taxi pulled into the station. I went outside and asked the driver if he would take me home. He agreed, and the attendant let me leave my car on his lot.

When the taxi driver pulled up in front of my home, he told me the fare was $15. I handed him a hundred-dollar bill and told him to keep the change. When I went back to the gas station a few days later, I also gave the manager another hundred-dollar bill and asked him to share it with the attendant who had been so kind. Those were the best two hundred dollars I could have spent.

While I didn't need to be that generous, it was something I wanted to do. In travel emergencies, it is always good to have cash because it gives you options that plastic may not provide.

Instant Gratification

A stockbroker told me how she used to tell her children they were going on an adventure when they were little. She'd tell each of them to grab a T-shirt and a toothbrush and to get in the car. She and her husband would drive their kids somewhere, usually to the Eastern Shore of Maryland, and stay overnight in a hotel. "But we'll have to wear the same underwear and socks," her kids complained.

"Yes, that's part of the adventure," was her answer.

She also told me how, when she was younger, she would travel without advance planning. "If I had thought about it, I wouldn't have done it. After all, it was stupid flying across the Atlantic, just going for the weekend to see a guy I thought I liked. But you can't think too much."

One of the things I know for a fact is that the things you most regret are those you don't go after, or don't try for, or don't do. That sums up my approach to travel.

Now the stockbroker has a fantasy of going to a nearby airport and just getting on a plane to somewhere. "If I didn't have a husband and kids, or if I could talk my husband into it, I would do it.

"He would probably get into it," she added. "He might need some pushing. But he doesn't like to plan things so it might be fun for him from that standpoint. It would be a ton of fun. I have a whole list of things I want to do and places I want to go.

"When one of my daughters was nine years old, I asked her what she'd like to do. She said, 'I want to grow up to pay my taxes.' She wanted to do adult things.

"On my own list, I used to say I wanted to go on an African safari. Now I want to go to Morocco. I have a fascination with it."

Delayed Gratification

Earlier I talked about not going anywhere that you can't afford. That is not to suggest that you should forego traveling somewhere you truly want to go, or miss out going someplace to try something you truly want to try, whether that is on the Colorado River, the beaches of Rio, or the streets of Beijing.

This section is called delayed gratification. That is a misnomer, for planning and saving and dreaming about travel builds anticipation.

Another approach is to review where you want to go and what you want to do and see if there is a less expensive way to realize your travel dream without going on credit. That may include staying in a clean but less luxurious hotel, flying to an alternate airport, going for a shorter length of time, or going at a different time, somewhat off-season for that part of the world.

I'm not suggesting you travel in the midst of a hurricane or tornado, or that you wander around Paris in the snow. (Actually, this happened to me in early April once, so planning isn't always the answer. By going that time of year, I thought I would experience spring weather. I remember being cold because I hadn't brought the right clothes. But so what—I was in Paris, and it turned out to be great fun.)

Instead of going to a beach in the heat of the summer, there are, what is called in the travel industry, shoulder seasons—on either side of the high season—when the weather generally allows for outdoor activities but is usually less than ideal or prime.

I actually love going to the beach off-season, even if it is too cold to swim. I love having the surroundings seemingly to myself. It is at such times that I am tempted to keep my spiritual or meditative journal. It is also at such times that I take stock and plan the next act of my life.

In a "less expensive than I'd like but at least I won't be reminded of my trip every month when the credit card bills arrive" version of travel, another important factor is to budget for food. There's no reason you can't grab a sandwich somewhere and eat outside (weather permitting) at lunchtime, or eat your largest meal at lunchtime in a culture like Spain or Portugal where the largest meal of the day is often lunch anyway. Using this strategy saves money because dinner is generally more expensive; you can still have a light, inexpensive dinner and not go to bed hungry.

Besides, it is physically better to eat a heavier meal early in the day so you have time to burn off the calories.

You may also want to resist the urge to buy too many souvenirs. If your best friend's or spouse's birthday is coming up, by all means, buy something while you're away. Or buy something and put it away for an upcoming occasion.

I love giving people gifts. Once I buy someone something, however, I have trouble standing the suspense until I can give the gift to its recipient. I don't want to wait to see if my idea for the perfect thought was a good idea or not, and I want to see the person's reaction. I suppose this drama means that buying a gift for someone is as much a gift for me as it is for the recipient.

Still, when traveling, it is important to collect something for yourself too. My mom bought my dad and brother expensive gifts when she traveled with me to Europe. She bought me expensive gifts too, even though I was with her. For herself, she bought only a few inexpensive items and collected matchbooks from everywhere we went. Those matchbooks were in a top drawer when she died.

I wish I could go back and have a "do over" so I could buy her something special while we were there, but even though I was grown, I was still playing the part of daughter and didn't, quite frankly, think of it—though I realize that our trip together was a mutual gift of time and shared joy.

One time, I came home from San Francisco with a pretty blue nightgown that I had bought for myself. Mom really liked it and she asked me, next time I found something special like that for myself, to get her one too. I started doing that and really enjoyed it.

Now that she's gone, I miss "buying two" of things, so I've taken to "buying two" anyway and giving one to my young niece—to pass on the tradition that occurred rather happenstance, from a blue nightgown purchased in San Francisco. The nightgown is long worn out and thrown away, but I will never forget how it looked or what it meant.

While I'm suggesting that you curb your desire to overbuy, I do believe in shopping while traveling. Although I don't particularly like to shop when I'm home, on the road, I see things differently and find I am more interested in capturing the feelings of travel and the auras of the places I visit. I recommend you do the same.

A matchbook, shot glass, or a menu can mean just as much, maybe more, than expensive rubies still being paid for a couple decades later. Capture the essence of your trip; don't go into debt to do it. A little imagination can lead to creative keepsakes. It is the memories, after all, that constitute the important part. It is the intrinsic, not the monetary value, that is significant.

Argentina, Belize, and Costa Rica

In many ways, the world is shrinking. We can call, e-mail, and text anywhere within seconds. We have access to quicker travel than at any time in human history (unless there are delays and other snafus). And yet it is a big world, with more in it than any one of us can personally get to know. Even living in a place your entire life—unless it is a very small town and perhaps even then—you never get to know all there is to know.

Maybe because I am so enamored by traveling, so determined to satisfy my curiosity by seeing and experiencing things for myself, that I seem to attract friends with similar interests. Through these friends, I expand the number of places I am receptive to visiting.

Someone asked if I'm interested in attending a food and wine event in Buenos Aires next year. Because I have two sets of friends who already visited there, it is more appealing as I already have a personal connection, once or twice removed.

A friend suggested Belize to me a few years ago as a great place to go deep-sea fishing. While I've never been deep-sea fishing, now whenever I see anything about Belize, I read it with interest. I won't be surprised to find myself there one day soon.

Another friend told me how he went to Costa Rica and tried zip-lining (sliding along a suspended cable to access something like a rainforest canopy). I haven't made up my mind about this one yet, but I'm interested in finding out what you need to wear and the best places to go before I decide.

If you're trekking somewhere, try to find someone . . . a friend of a friend of a friend . . . who's already tried whatever it is you're planning to try, or visited wherever it is you're planning to go. The conversation could prove beneficial.

It's Not Important Where You Go

. . . or even for how long. What *is* important is that you enjoy the experience, that it's special to you. The art of traveling solo is finding the perfect experience for yourself. You don't have to consult anyone or cater to anyone. You don't have the luxury of leaving it up to someone else—only you can decide what to eat and where to sleep. Only you know what it really means.

When my dad died, I felt lost for a long time. He was, in many ways, my confidant. I could tell him anything, knowing that he would never betray my trust. I was used to sharing my travels with him, discussing what I learned and how it felt.

After he died, I searched for someone else in whom I could confide. In some ways, a few friends fill that role. In other ways, no one else ever will. So I have learned to live for myself in a way I never did when there was someone who always understood. There are travels I take now, that are just for me.

Selecting a Destination

If I tell you there is no science to selecting a destination, that it's serendipity, it's happenstance, it's luck—whether good or bad—you may not believe me.

People are always asking me to tell them about my favorite place. Since I'm a travel writer, they figure I'll have an answer to this one ultimate travel question. In truth, my favorite place is the next place I'm going—preferably somewhere I've never been before.

I do like returning to places I've been before, because I never rush around trying to see everything and do everything. Instead, I slow down and enjoy what I'm doing rather than trying to rack up points for seeing and doing the most things. If I return to a place, there are always new things to try or see. If I never go back, at least I enjoyed my time there.

But it's the anticipation of someplace new—a place I've heard about or read about or maybe know nothing at all about—that truly excites me.

Although everyone wants an answer, I'll give you a list of questions to ask yourself instead. At the end of this easy, self-study exercise, you should have a good idea where to go. If not, tape a map of the world onto the wall, close your eyes, and throw a dart. Consider going wherever the dart lands. But since you're traveling alone, no one needs to know that once you opened your eyes, you cheated and moved the dart. My bet is on that happening—that you'll move the dart because there's someplace you'd rather go than where the dart lands. We'll keep that between us; it will be our little secret.

Ask Yourself the Following Questions:

1. If you'll be someplace on business, will it work to add days onto the trip for some leisure pursuits?
2. Do you prefer to stay in the U.S. or travel to other countries?
3. If you want to stay in the U.S. or time is limited, are there specific regions of the country that you prefer? If so, maybe you should go to a different one, just for the fun of it.
4. What is the planned length of your trip—four days, one week, ten days, two weeks?
5. Are there limits on the amount of money to be spent? This may have an impact on the luxuriousness of the spa/resort/hotel/flight, but not necessarily on how much fun you're going to have. Some of my favorite trips have been to not-so-exclusive places. In fact, oftentimes you meet more people at a communal breakfast in a B&B than you do in a luxury hotel where everyone has breakfast sent up to their suite.
6. Are there any sports you particularly enjoy, such as golf, tennis, snorkeling, hang gliding, fishing, or horseback riding?
7. Are you looking for quiet or excitement?
8. What do you generally like to do at home on the weekend?
9. What kinds of trips have you taken previously? What did you like and dislike about them?
10. Is there something you've always wanted to do but have been putting off, for whatever reason? (This is the best question of all.)

Deciding on a Trip

With so many options from which to choose, you can do research through books and the Internet, and you can also talk to everyone you know. Yet at some point, you need to make a decision.

If you're tacking on leisure to a business trip, your general destination is predetermined.

Just remember that travel is often best when we go without expectations. Then we can enjoy whatever we find rather than looking for something that's probably not there, at least in the form we expected.

People travel for different reasons and each experience is unique to its participant. For me, learning about a new area, understanding the people who come from that area and their concerns and viewpoints, widens my perspective.

After all, a traveler is never quite the same after a new experience, a new place that's been visited.

Travel as Its Own Reward

Many travel-related activities come with points. I call serious business travelers "road warrior points junkies." Often, when sitting and having dinner with these road warriors in a hotel restaurant, the conversation invariably turns to which hotel chain is giving extra points that week, or the rules for checking in and checking out and then in again, so as to get extra benefits.

The perks from rental car companies, credit card charges, hotels, airlines, even coffee shops that give out a free latte after purchase of a dozen, are just whipped cream on top of the great sundae of your experiences. To follow the analogy to its logical conclusion, getting to a cherry involves a lot of travel.

Leslie's Rule

When I was in third grade, my teacher, Mrs. Luray, taught us the Luray Law: "When you add dollars and cents, you don't get cats and dogs."

I'll never forget this rule. As a result, I always put a dollar sign in front of amounts of money, even when I fill in the amount I'm paying on a bill remittance slip.

I don't remember my other elementary teachers' names, but I'll never forget Mrs. Luray. She left an indelible impression because she gave us a rule.

So here, at the end of my book on solo travel, is my rule for use on all your journeys: "Leslie's rule is that there are no rules. Forge your own path."

All I can give you are ideas and stories—my ideas and my stories, along with some I've collected from others along the way. Use these as a point of departure. Challenge yourself in your own way, enjoy yourself in ways that are unique to you.

In the process, you will discover a bit more about this world of ours. You will discover a bit more about yourself too, and your place in this world.

Unlike Mrs. Luray's law, travel is not something that can be measured in dollars and cents. Travel may cost money, but its measurement is elusive; it is something special that changes you, enlightens you, gives you a wider perspective.

Sometimes you recognize the significance of a particular trip. Sometimes, it's just part of the fabric of experiences that defines you. Sometimes the effect is specific. At other times, it's just inexplicably great fun.

I definitely recommend that you go out and explore. If you run into a rock star or a politician along the way, say hello. Whenever you meet someone, strike up a conversation. Ask questions. Have a dialogue. Witness something new. Enjoy the scenery. Take mental note. Feel your emotions. Or just play the role of observer.

If you're fortunate, you may uncover what truly captivates you. Just remember that the journey is inevitably more important than the destination. Not everyone finds nirvana, but it is the process of going on the search that matters.

As one of my favorite friends always tells me,
"Safe travels."

ONLINE TRAVEL RESOURCES

The proliferation of useful travel sites is a great source of riches. Most people, especially those who travel a lot, have their favorites. I polled several in-the-know travelers, added sites I regularly use, and compiled this list as a jumping off point.

Search Tips
- ✔ google.com—great place to start for just about anything

- ✔ convention and visitors bureaus (CVB)—in the google.com search bar, enter the name of a U.S. city followed by the acronym CVB

- ✔ tourist boards and offices—in the google.com search bar, enter the name of a country followed by "tourist board" or "tourist office"

Comparisons
- kayak.com—airfares and hotel rates
- mobissimo.com—airfares and hotel rates
- sidestep.com—airfares and hotel rates

Flights
- farecast.com—predicts fare increases or decreases
- infoairports.com—links to airport websites
- low-cost-airline-guide.com—European routes
- seatguru.com—aircraft configuration for help with seat selection
- . . . also check individual airline sites

Hotels

- bedandbreakfast.com—by destination
- lhw.com—the Leading Hotels of the World (luxury)
- tripadvisor.com—hotel reviews by travelers
- . . . also check individual hotel sites

Maps and Driving

- aaa.com—driving directions and travel guides
- mapquest.com—maps and driving directions
- maps.google.com—allows you to see exactly where you're going
- . . . also check individual rental car sites

Rail Travel

- amtrak.com—U.S. rail
- raileurope.com—European rail

Security Information

- safetravel.dot.gov—U.S. Department of Transportation
- travel.state.gov—U.S. Department of State (travel warnings and alerts plus passports for U.S. citizens)
- tsa.dhs.gov—Transportation Security Administration

Specialty

- lastminute.com—last minute travel (by country)
- luxurylink.com—auction style
- opentable.com—dining/restaurant reservations
- xe.com—currency conversions

Time and Weather

- timeanddate.com—time zones
- weather.com—forecasts

ABOUT THE AUTHOR

Portofino, Italy

Leslie Atkins is an award-winning writer with a keen knack for observation and an ability to evoke emotion—her own and that of her readers. She began her career in journalism as a television writer for Oprah Winfrey. Then she started writing weekend getaway stories for the *Washington Post* and quickly discovered an immense passion for travel and adventure.

Leslie's writing has appeared in *USA Today, Car & Travel, AAA World, US Airways Magazine*, the *Baltimore Sun, Pittsburgh Post-Gazette*, and many other publications. She particularly loves to share the excitement that comes from travel, and her favorite place is the next place she's going—preferably somewhere she's never been before.

Her passions include tennis, college basketball, golden retrievers, books, and art. Leslie also loves visiting new places, trying new sports, and talking with people to learn their stories. It is in the stories that the richness of life reveals itself to her, and Leslie constantly searches for anecdotes, ideas, and provocative thoughts to share with readers.

Leslie received her Bachelor of Arts in History and English from the University of Maryland, College Park, where she is a member of Phi Beta Kappa. She owns a writing and editorial services firm with a national clientele, and she frequently speaks at such venues as the National Press Club, association conferences, and universities.